STUDENT UNIT GUIDE

AS Psychology
UNIT 2

Individual Differences,
Physiology and Behaviour

Christine Brain

AS Psychology

Philip Allan Updates
Market Place
Deddington
Oxfordshire
OX15 0SE

tel: 01869 338652
fax: 01869 337590
e-mail: sales@philipallan.co.uk
www.philipallan.co.uk

© Philip Allan Updates 2003

ISBN-13: 978-0-86003-885-6
ISBN-10: 0-86003-885-8

All rights reserved; no part of this publication may be reproduced, stored in a retrieval system, or transmitted, in any form or by any means, electronic, mechanical, photocopying, recording or otherwise without either the prior written permission of Philip Allan Updates or a licence permitting restricted copying in the United Kingdom issued by the Copyright Licensing Agency Ltd, 90 Tottenham Court Road, London W1P 9HE.

This Guide has been written specifically to support students preparing for the Edexcel AS Psychology Unit 2 examination. The content has been neither approved nor endorsed by Edexcel and remains the sole responsibility of the author.

Printed by Information Press, Eynsham, Oxford

Environmental information
The paper on which this title is printed is sourced from managed, sustainable forests.

Contents

Introduction
About this guide 4
Study skills and revision strategies 5
Examination structure and skills 8

■ ■ ■

Content Guidance
About this section 14
The learning approach
Two key assumptions 15
Research methods used in the learning approach 15
In-depth areas of study 18
Two studies in detail 24
Key application: the deliberate alteration of human behaviour 28
Contemporary issue: the effects of violence on television 30
Summary of the learning approach 31
The psychodynamic approach
Two key assumptions 32
Research methods used in the psychodynamic approach 32
In-depth areas of study 36
Two studies in detail 41
Key application: understanding mental health issues 44
Contemporary issue: false-memory syndrome 46
Summary of the psychodynamic approach 47
The physiological approach
Two key assumptions 47
Research methods used in the physiological approach 48
In-depth areas of study 52
Two studies in detail 55
Key application: circadian rhythms, shiftwork and jet lag 58
Contemporary issue: the 24-hour society 60
Summary of the physiological approach 61

■ ■ ■

Questions and Answers
About this section 64
Section 1 The learning approach 65
Section 2 The psychodynamic approach 74
Section 3 The physiological approach 82

AS Psychology

Introduction

About this guide

This is a guide to Unit 2 of the Edexcel AS specification. Before looking at what this guide is all about, here is some good news (in the form of positive reinforcement). You can pass the exam for this unit, and you can do well. How can I draw this conclusion without knowing you? Because you are reading this guide.

Students who take the trouble to read this sort of guide:
- are motivated to do well
- have an idea about where to look for help
- understand what unit they are taking, and with which examination board
- know something about active learning — we can learn better if we engage in tasks, such as using this sort of student guide

So you already have some of the skills and knowledge you need — hence my claim that you can do well. However, this guide:
- is not a textbook — there is no substitute for reading the required material and taking notes
- does not tell you the actual questions on your paper, or give you the answers!

Aims

The aim of this guide is to provide you with a clear understanding of the requirements of Unit 2 of the AS specification and to advise you on how best to meet these requirements.

This guide will look at:
- the psychology you need to know about
- what you need to be able to do and what skills you need
- how you could go about learning the necessary material
- what is being examined
- what you should expect in the examination
- how you could tackle the different styles of exam question
- the format of the exam, including what questions might look like
- how questions are marked, including examples of answers, with examiner's comments

How to use this guide

A good way to use this guide is to read it through in the order in which it is presented. Alternatively, you can consider each topic in the Content Guidance section, and then turn to the relevant question in the Question and Answer section.

Whichever way you use the guide, try some of the questions yourself to test your learning. Hopefully, you will know enough about the marking by this time to try to grade your own answers. If you are working with someone else, mark each other's answers.

The more you work on what is needed, the better. Have your textbooks available too — you will need access to all the relevant information.

Study skills and revision strategies

If you have been studying the Unit 2 material, and have engaged in a reasonable amount of learning up to now, you can make good use of this guide.

This guide can also help if you know very little of the material and have only a short time before the examination. If this describes you, you have a lot of work and long hours of study ahead — but you can do it.

Before reading on, answer the following questions:
- How long is left before the exam?
- Do you have a revision plan?
- Are you sure you want to pass, and hopefully do well? Renewing your motivation can help.
- Are you stressed and in a panic?
- Can you stick to your plan, and trust it?

If you need to, draw up a revision plan now, remind yourself that you want to succeed, and practise some relaxation techniques.

How to learn the material

- Make notes, but be concise and use your own notes for final revision.
- Have a separate sheet of paper for each approach.
- For each approach, note down the six headings (see the summary at the end of each approach) and use that as a guide. Leave room to fit your notes in under each heading.
- Read through each section, then make notes as needed (very briefly).
- Be sure to make notes on evaluation points.
- Finally, note down briefly three things about a contemporary issue that describe the issue, and six 'facts' linking concepts to the issue.

Another useful method is to use cards for each topic. Have the topic heading on one side of the card and brief notes on the other. Remember to note down equal amounts of knowledge and evaluation.

Revision plan

- Start at least 4 weeks before the exam date (sooner if possible).
- Using times that suit you (6 a.m. might be a great time to study!), draw up a blank timetable for each of the weeks.
- On the timetable, fill in all your urgent commitments (cancel as many plans as you can).
- Divide up what is left, allocating slots to all your subjects as appropriate. Don't forget to build in meal times, breaks and time for sleep.
- Stick to the plan if at all possible, but if you have to, amend it as you go.
- When studying, have frequent, short rests, and no distractions.

Time management

Answer the following questions to see how good you are at time management:

(1) Are you usually punctual?
   yes   no

(2) Do you tend to work fast and then correct mistakes?
   yes   no

(3) Do you often put things off?
   yes   no

(4) Do you feel stressed because you never have enough time?
   yes   no

(5) Do you work slowly and carefully, and try to get things right first time?
   yes   no

(6) Do you daydream?
   yes   no

(7) Are you forgetful?
   yes   no

(8) Do you find it hard to get started?
   yes   no

(9) Do you keep your desk tidy?
   yes   no

Score 0 for 'yes' and 1 for 'no' to questions 1, 5 and 9. Score 1 for 'yes' and 0 for 'no' to questions 2, 3, 4, 6, 7 and 8. A score of 3 or below means quite good time management; a score of 4 and above means you need to work on it.

Relaxation techniques

Boxes 1, 2 and 3 suggest ways to relax. Use these as appropriate.

Box 1: Technique 1 — takes about 10 minutes

This technique is useful at the start or at the end of a longish revision period.

- Sit on the floor and make yourself comfortable.
- Working from toes to head, tense each of your muscles in turn and then relax.
- Having relaxed your body, now relax your thoughts.
- Take yourself in your mind to a place where you feel at peace — this could be a favourite holiday place, or a favourite place on a walk. Closing your eyes will help.
- Have a good look around (mentally!), sit down there and hear the sounds of the place.
- Stay there and try not to come back yet.
- When you are ready, come back. Slowly start to hear the sounds around you, and lie with your body relaxed for a little while longer.

Box 2: Technique 2 — takes about 5 minutes

This technique is useful as you revise. Work for between 30 minutes and an hour, and then stop to relax as follows:

- Sit comfortably and try to ignore anything going on around you.
- Imagine you are in a barn, sitting on the rafters under the roof, swinging your legs and sitting comfortably. Closing your eyes will help.
- Now, imagine that the barn has open doors at both ends, and there is a river rushing through from one end of the barn to the other. You are sitting swinging your legs, watching the river rush through below you.
- Hear the water rushing through, sit comfortably, and just watch.
- Think of the water as your thoughts rushing away.
- You are not involved, just watching.
- After about 3 minutes or when you are ready, slowly start to hear the sounds around you, and gradually bring your thoughts back into the real world. Look around you for a minute or two and check that you feel better, before getting back to work.

Box 3: Technique 3 — takes about 1 minute

This technique is useful when you are actually in the examination, and can be used if you are too anxious to continue.

- Imagine you are in an exam now.
- Imagine that you are getting anxious.
- Pick up a pen as if to write.
- Hold the pen up in front of you and stare at it.
- Let all your other thoughts go and think about the pen.
- Try to think of nothing else even for a few seconds.
- Get back to work!

Examination structure and skills

Unit 2 consists of six main questions, ranging across the three approaches. There are two questions for each approach, although marks are not evenly distributed between the approaches. The aim is to ask questions covering the six areas within the approaches, as well as the three approaches themselves. For example, if you are asked a question about common research methods in the learning approach, you are unlikely to be asked a 'method' question for the other approaches. Remember the six main areas: two key assumptions; research methods; in-depth areas of study; two studies in detail; one key application; and one contemporary issue. The three approaches for Unit 2 are the learning approach, the psychodynamic approach and the physiological approach. You need to be prepared to answer a question on any of the six main areas for each of the three approaches.

Each exam paper has reasonably straightforward questions at the start, leading to an extended writing question (essay question) at the end. Don't think that someone sets each paper with past papers in front of them, avoiding what has been asked before. Imagine someone trying to set an interesting paper, covering the six areas, ranging across the approaches, and balancing AO1 and AO2 marks according to the required percentages of each. It is not possible to guess what will be on the paper — don't try. Prepare answers for all possible questions. The only guarantee is that there will be an essay question at the end of each paper, and the mark allocation for that essay will be 10 or 12 marks.

Different people set the papers, and there are not as many strict rules as you might think. Tips in this guide include words such as 'usually'. Each paper will be different, and you have to be prepared to answer whatever questions appear. For example, there are many ways that a table can be presented, and you can be asked to tick statements, cross false statements, join correct claims together and so on. Read the question carefully and do what is asked, and you will do well.

Assessment objectives

The assessment objectives are listed in the specification. A brief explanation is given below, but check the full list of what you will be assessed on.

Assessment Objective 1: knowledge and understanding (AO1)
- You need to explain your knowledge and understanding of psychological terminology and concepts through appropriate use and application.
- You must demonstrate knowledge and understanding of psychological theories, studies, methods and concepts, as well as psychological principles, perspectives and applications.
- You must communicate clearly and effectively, and present and select material well. For example, if you are asked to give a weakness of experiments and you

say they are not valid, this does not get a mark, as you have not shown any understanding (although you have shown knowledge). You need to make the point clearly — for example, experiments are not valid as they do not take place in a natural setting. You may lose marks by using bullet points, so avoid them. The problem with bullet points is that they encourage short-hand, meaning that your answer will not be clearly and effectively communicated.

Assessment Objective 2: evaluation and comment (AO2)
You must be able to:
- analyse and evaluate psychological theories and concepts, referring to relevant evidence
- appraise psychological studies and methods

Assessment Objective 3 (AO3)
Assessment Objective 3 is examined in Units 3 and 5, and is not dealt with here.

The Unit 2 exam

Unit 2 is assessed in a 90-minute exam. Answers are written in a booklet similar to those used at GCSE, and you can use spare paper too. 72 marks are available. This means you need to score around 1 mark per minute, with 18 minutes to spare for reading and thinking. In general, you can expect to gain 1 mark for each point that answers the question, or for elaboration of a point. Answers must be communicated 'clearly and effectively' (see AO1 above). Avoid one-word answers unless they are asked for. The final essay question is worth 10 or 12 marks. Overall, approximately 42 marks are awarded for knowledge and understanding (AO1) and 30 marks for evaluation and comment (AO2).

Essay mark scheme
Essay questions are likely to be about a key application or a contemporary issue, but other areas may be tested.

Essays have 2 marks (AO1 marks) available for clarity and communication (use of terms, spelling and ways of expressing points) and 2 marks (AO2 marks) for balance and breadth. In addition, for a 10-mark essay you need to give three AO1 'knowledge and understanding' points and three AO2 'evaluation and comment' points. For a 12-mark essay, four AO1 points, and four AO2 points, are required.

AO1 and AO2: getting it right
You must be sure to answer the question that is set — you should then cover the AO1 and AO2 skills. The key words in the question (called **injunctions**) guide what you need to write. If you answer the question, you will automatically do what is required. Table 1 shows some examples of how AO1 injunctions are used and Table 2 shows examples of AO2 injunctions. Note that it is not so much the word itself (e.g. 'describe') that makes it AO1 or AO2, as the whole question. The figures in brackets suggest the mark allocation you might expect for such a question.

Table 1 Examples of AO1 questions/injunctions

Type of question	What is being asked for
Describe a theory… (4)	Say what something is (a theory in this case). Imagine describing the theory to someone who knows little about the subject.
Identify a theory… (1)	Give enough information so that the examiner can understand what is being referred to. For example, if asked to identify a memory theory, the answer might be 'working memory model'.
Name a theory… (1)	Name either the theory or the psychologist(s). For example, if the question asks for a memory theory, the answer might be Atkinson and Shiffrin's or the two-stage model.
Outline an assumption… (3)	Follow the instructions for 'describe', but remember that this injunction usually requires less detail, and hence carries fewer marks.
Describe a study… (5)	Try to give the aim of the study, the method, the procedure, the results and the conclusion(s).

Table 2 Examples of AO2 questions/injunctions

Type of question	What is being asked for
Outline a strength of… (2)	You are asked to outline something, so the injunction seems to be AO1 (i.e. knowledge and understanding). However, as what is outlined is a *strength* (in this case), and thus you are being asked to evaluate something, this question would carry AO2 marks.
Evaluate a study… (5)	Give comments, criticisms, good points and so on about a study. Consider strengths and weaknesses of the method, perhaps, or criticisms of the ethics involved. Look at alternative findings or consider whether justified conclusions are drawn.
Explain, using learning theory concepts… (6)	Use concepts within learning theory (e.g. positive and negative reinforcement) to explain something. So you would say how something happens by reference to positive reinforcement, for example.
Assess the effect of… (4)	Show what the effect of something is (e.g. use of cognitive developmental theory in education) and then suggest to what extent this is useful (assess).

AO1 and AO2: injunctions in essay questions

Essay questions will always involve equal marks for AO1 and AO2. You should demonstrate knowledge and understanding and provide comment and evaluation. Remember spelling and use of terminology (2 AO1 marks for clarity and communication). Remember to address all parts of the question (2 AO2 marks for breadth and balance). Table 3 shows the importance of knowing how AO1 and AO2 marks are split in each examination paper (excluding Unit 3, the coursework element).

Edexcel Unit 2

Table 3 Approximate mark allocation AO1/AO2

	AO1	AO2	Total
AS Units 1 and 2	42	30	72
A2 Units 4 and 5a*	28	44	72
A2 Unit 6	36	36	72

* Unit 5b has an AO3 (experiment/investigation) component

Table 3 shows how, for the two AS units, you will be assessed more on your knowledge and understanding (58%) than on your ability to comment and evaluate (42%). However, for two of the A2 units, you will be assessed more on your ability to comment and evaluate (61%) than on your knowledge and understanding (39%). For Unit 6, your knowledge and understanding and your evaluation and comment skills are assessed equally.

Essentially, then, you have to learn the material so that you know and understand it, and then plan some criticisms, comments and evaluation points. As a rule of thumb, be sure to learn or plan as many evaluation and comment points as you learn information points.

Conclusions: use of injunctions and the AO1/AO2 split

Don't just think of a word in the question as being the whole question. For example, 'describe' is an AO1 command, but 'describe a strength...' is an AO2 injunction. 'Discuss' could signal AO2 marks if you are asked to 'discuss the usefulness of...' Because you are considering how useful something is, you are doing more than showing knowledge about it. The best approach is to *answer the question*. If you study and understand the question, all should be well.

This section provides an overview of what you need to learn for Unit 2. Remember, you need access to more material than is given here.

An attempt is made to balance presenting knowledge with giving suggestions for evaluation. Remember the rule of thumb — you must prepare equal amounts of AO1 and AO2 material.

Structure of the AS units

Each unit comprises three of the main approaches in psychology. Each approach follows the same format:
- two key assumptions (your choice)
- research methods used (some specified ones)
- in-depth areas of study (specified)
- two studies in detail (your choice)
- one key application (specified)
- one contemporary issue (your choice)

Unit 2 covers learning, psychodynamic and physiological approaches.

As you can see, for some areas of Unit 2 you can choose what you study. In this section suitable material is presented, but you may well have studied different examples.

The learning approach

Two key assumptions

Our environment shapes our behaviour

Environmental factors act as stimuli, and we learn to respond to them. An example of how this learning works is positive reinforcement. If our response provides something pleasant, then we repeat our response. This does not take into account our genetic make-up. All learning comes from responding to our environment and through our experiences.

Behaviour is measurable

We can set up a stimulus and observe and measure the response. This means that learning theory, with its emphasis on overt behaviour, can be studied scientifically. This in turn can lead to general laws about our behaviour.

Summary

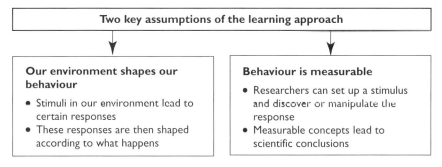

Research methods used in the learning approach

Laboratory experiments

Experiments take place in controlled conditions, where one variable (the independent variable, IV) is manipulated (changed) in some way to see the effect of this manipulation (change) on another variable (the dependent variable, DV). From this manipulation, a cause-and-effect relationship can often be claimed.

For example, Bandura, Ross and Ross (1961) set up a situation in which children watched adults 'beating' a bobo doll (an inflatable toy, around 120 cm tall, which stands on a weighted base and will return to a standing position on being punched), or playing in other ways. Some children watched the aggressive behaviour while others watched an adult behaving in a non-aggressive way. There were a number of different conditions but, basically, the independent variable was whether the adult was aggressive or not, and the dependent variable was whether the children then imitated the adult's actions when playing with a bobo doll themselves. By carefully controlling a number of factors (e.g. the age of the child or what they watched), a cause-and-effect relationship was concluded: if young children watch adults behaving aggressively, they are likely to imitate that aggression.

> **Evaluation**
> + Variables other than the IV and the DV are tightly controlled, so cause-and-effect conclusions can be drawn. If only the IV changes, and something changes in the DV, we can say that the IV change(s) *caused* the change in the DV. Good controls tend to mean good reliability.
> − The IV has to be singled out and all variables controlled. This means that often the situation is very unusual, and only one variable (the IV) is looked at. In real life, things that vary about people are not all separate or measurable in this way. Because of this, experiments are often said to lack validity.

Animal learning studies

Animals are often studied in the learning approach, partly because isolating a stimulus to measure a response is easier with animals than with humans. Animals can be used in a laboratory setting or they can be observed in a more natural setting. In both cases, animal studies tend to be experiments. Even when using a natural setting, the researcher may manipulate the situation, and the study is therefore a field experiment.

Animals in laboratory studies

An example of using animals in laboratory experiments is Pavlov's study with dogs. His study of how dogs learn to salivate at the sight of a laboratory assistant (because he or she brings food) was well controlled. The salivation was measured precisely. The pairing of the laboratory assistant and the food had happened naturally, but other studies were done with careful controls to show that there was a cause-and-effect relationship between the association (pairing) and the response.

> **Evaluation**
> + Animals are easier to use than humans because of ethical issues. There are those who would not agree, but ethical guidelines regarding animals are more flexible than those concerning humans.
> + Most animals are easier to study because of their smaller size, while their ability to breed quickly means that large numbers can be studied and links with nature or nurture assessed more easily.
> − Findings from a study done on one species of animals cannot be generalised to another species, including humans.

– Different animals (including humans) have different cognitive capabilities, which makes generalising from one species to another difficult.

Animal field studies

Other studies on animals are done in the animal's natural habitat. For example, behaviourists like Watson watched birds and observed their habits. He tried to see what was learned by the birds and what behaviour was innate. In one experiment, he moved a bird's nest a very short distance away and yet the bird still returned to where the nest had been, and even made movements as if settling down on a nest. Watson concluded that birds use landmarks to learn where their nest is, and that they have little flexibility in 'realising' that the nest has been moved.

When watching animals in a natural setting, researchers observe and make notes a lot of the time, but they also carry out experiments like the one described above, so they can isolate the behaviour to be measured.

Evaluation

+ Because these studies are done in a natural setting, the findings are valid up to a point. They have ecological validity in the sense of the setting being appropriate. However, there are validity problems, as outlined below.
+ As there is often manipulation, the studies can be replicated and the same results found, so they are reliable.
− There can be validity problems because of manipulation. For example, in the study outlined above, the bird's nest was moved. This would not normally happen, so whatever behaviour was observed was not natural.
− Results are found by observation, and researchers can be biased when observing, as there is an element of interpretation.

Summary

Two research methods commonly used in the learning approach

Laboratory experiments
IV is manipulated, DV is measured; other variables are controlled

Advantages
- Cause-and-effect relationship studied
- Can be repeated (good controls)
- Good reliability

Disadvantages
- Control of variables means not real life
- Poor validity

Animal learning studies
Laboratory studies
Advantages
- Controls; easy to handle animals

Disadvantages
- Generalising is difficult
- Ethical issues

Field studies
Advantages
- Valid, as in natural setting

Disadvantages
- Still some manipulation, so some question over validity
- Some ethical issues

AS Psychology

In-depth areas of study

For each of the three types of learning specified (**classical conditioning**, **operant conditioning** and **social learning theory**) you need to be able to:
- describe the mechanisms
- give one example of its use in humans
- evaluate the type of learning as an explanation of human behaviour

Classical conditioning

Mechanisms of classical conditioning

A natural stimulus leads to a reflex response. Classical conditioning only applies to reflexive, natural responses, not to artificially learnt behaviour such as washing the car. For example, food leads to salivation, or blowing on the eye leads to blinking. These reactions are reflexes, and are unavoidable and involuntary. When trying to work out if learning is classical or operant conditioning, consider the response and see if it occurs naturally and unavoidably after the stimulus. These natural responses can be associated with a different stimulus by association learning — this is classical conditioning.

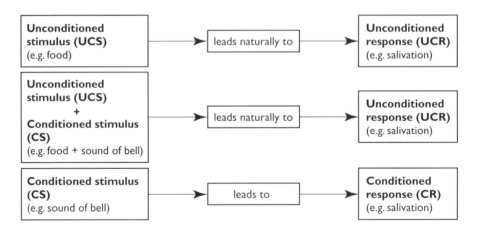

- **Extinction** occurs if the UCS and the CS are not paired for a little while (e.g. the bell rings without food being brought).
- **Generalisation** means learning to associate a similar stimulus (e.g. a similar sounding bell) with the CR (e.g. salivation).
- **Discrimination** means learning to associate only a particular stimulus (e.g. only one type of bell) with the CR.
- **Spontaneous recovery** refers to an occasion when a CR recurs in response to the CS even after extinction. For example, after a time of not ringing the bell with food being brought, the salivation response to the bell is extinguished. However, there can sometimes be spontaneous recovery of the salivation response to the bell ringing.

Edexcel Unit 2

> **Tip**
> Use Watson and Rayner's (1920) study to help with your understanding of classical conditioning. It is one of the 'studies in detail' and is outlined on pp. 24–26.

Classical conditioning in humans

Systematic desensitisation to reduce problems associated with phobias is a therapy derived from classical conditioning explanations. A phobia can be explained as a learned association between a conditioned stimulus and the conditioned response of fear. For example:

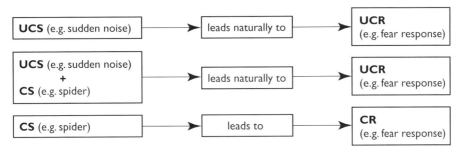

> **Evaluation**
> + Classical conditioning has been demonstrated in many different studies, so it looks as though results are reliable.
> + Practical applications, such as aversion therapy and systematic desensitisation, do seem to work (see below). When practical applications from a theory are found to have value, this suggests that the theory is valid.
> − Much of the research is carried out on animals. This means that the results should not be generalised to humans because of differences between animals and humans.
> − Classical conditioning mechanisms only explain how there is association between stimuli and reflexive actions. This does not explain all behaviours.

Based on the idea that we cannot feel two conflicting emotions (such as fear and relaxation) at one time, classical conditioning principles can be used to help a person learn a different response to the stimulus of the spider. For example:

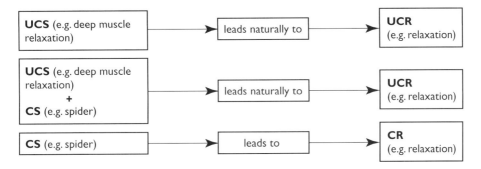

19

Features of systematic desensitisation include gradually introducing the actual feared object. For example, using a real spider immediately will give a strong fear response and may override the relaxation. The therapist might therefore use a picture of a spider initially, and gradually progress to a real spider. In this way, the relaxation response can be maintained and replaces the fear response.

Evaluation

+ Systematic desensitisation seems to work, but it is better for small phobias than for major ones, such as agoraphobia.
+ The success of the therapy is evidence that the phobia might have been caused by classical conditioning, although it is not proof.
- Those who benefit from systematic desensitisation tend to need a good imagination in order to maintain the relaxation response. They also have to transfer their learning to real-life situations, away from any institution where they might be receiving the treatment.
- It is often claimed that systematic desensitisation (and other behavioural therapies) is only a way of treating maladaptive behaviour and is not dealing with the cause of a problem such as a phobia. It is, perhaps, better used in conjunction with other types of therapy.
- It is only useful for problems that link to natural responses, such as a fear response, and does not work for all examples of maladaptive behaviour.

Operant conditioning

Mechanisms of operant conditioning

Operant conditioning, unlike classical conditioning, relates to voluntary behaviour, which means any behaviour other than reflexes. So, for operant conditioning, we have to produce the voluntary behaviour before it can be conditioned, and in research the behaviour cannot be elicited by a researcher. This means that someone's behaviour is either reinforced or punished, after it is exhibited. Positive reinforcement means a behaviour is encouraged in some way by providing something the individual sees as a treat or a good thing. Negative reinforcement means a behaviour is encouraged in order to avoid something the person sees as unpleasant. Punishment is used to stop a behaviour being carried out.

Reinforcers are classed as either primary or secondary. Primary reinforcers refer to anything that is desired for itself, such as heat, food and comfort — these are basic needs. Secondary reinforcers refer to anything that can be used to gain primary reinforcers, such as money or tokens. There are also different schedules of reinforcement, which concern the time between reinforcers and how often they are given.

An important part of operant conditioning is the idea of shaping. Different behaviours are shaped by reinforcing behaviour that works gradually towards the desired behaviour. For example, it is hard to get a squirrel to do an assault course, as an advertisement once portrayed. However, it can be done gradually, by getting the squirrel to do parts of the course and then shaping its behaviour until it has completed every stage.

Discrimination and generalisation apply in operant conditioning as well as in classical conditioning.

One example of operant conditioning in humans

One example of operant conditioning in humans is the way we learn language. All babies babble — we know this because cross-cultural studies show it clearly. They then learn their specific language, and learn to make the necessary sounds. In fact, the ability to make all sounds is lost. As they make sounds, they get excitement and response from their caregivers. These responses are positive reinforcement, because the baby likes the attention. Operant conditioning suggests that when we get a positive response for a behaviour, we do it again, so the baby is likely to make that sound again — for example, 'dada'. There is a two-way interaction in that the caregiver will reinforce the right sounds by their responses, and the baby will respond more to get this attention. Language is shaped by these reinforcement patterns. Those sounds not reinforced are the ones lost in the early months (first year).

Evaluation

+ Operant conditioning can account for how we learn many different behaviours, and seems like common-sense. We can relate to the idea, as we know that if something good comes from a behaviour, we are more likely to do it again. Most people know that if we reward a dog for something, it is likely to repeat the behaviour and look for the reward.
+ It is useful when applied to learning, as it shows that punishment is not as effective as using rewards. Punishment does not demonstrate the desired behaviour, and aggression can be modelled by the punisher, with negative consequences.
+ It is useful in schools and institutions and has given rise to therapies such as the token economy programme.
+ Operant conditioning does seem a good explanation of how we learn language, given what we know about the interactions between babies and their caregivers. A baby's first 'words' are a cause for excitement, and it makes sense that a baby will then repeat the sounds.
+ It helps to explain why children speak their own language very well, and how they are able to give all the necessary subtleties of sounds.
− Many studies looking at operant conditioning use animals. These are then generalised to humans. As animals are different in many ways from humans, generalising the results of these studies might not be desirable.
− Operant conditioning seems to explain many examples of learning. However, it does not consider other factors, such as genetic/biological ones.
− When learning language, children use words that are not reinforced, such as 'shoppies' or 'wented'. These examples suggest that children apply the rules of grammar without these rules having been reinforced. It is thought that we might have an innate language acquisition device, so operant conditioning does not explain completely how we learn our language.
− Adults do not always correct young children when they use grammar incorrectly, or reinforce correct grammar. So how do children learn the right grammar?

Social learning theory

Social learning theory builds on the idea of identification, and how a child might identify with a parent and be likely to imitate their behaviour. There is still the idea of learning through conditioning — social learning theory accepts that this is the case. However, social learning theory focuses more on how we learn moral and social behaviour.

Social learning theorists accept that there are cognitive processes involved in learning, and they add the idea that we also learn through modelling on others, and imitating what they do. This is observational learning. Bandura points out that we are unlikely to wait for someone to carry out an action and then reward them, as operant conditioning would suggest. Quite often, a person simply does something because they are copying someone else.

Mechanisms of social learning theory

Observational learning involves modelling and imitating. However, not all behaviours are modelled or imitated. It depends on the model and also on the consequences of the action. For example, if an action is punished, the observer is less likely to copy it. If an action is positively reinforced, the observer is more likely to copy it.

One example of where Bandura suggests learning has a cognitive element is when reinforcement is motivational — we imitate behaviour if we are motivated to do so by its likely consequences.

We use particular people as models — for example parents, those of the same gender, those similar to us, and those who have similar interests.

Cognitive factors that contribute to observational learning include:
- paying attention to the important parts of the action
- recording information in our memory
- having a well-organised memory
- motivation — the consequences decide if the behaviour is carried out or not

Use your chosen *study in detail* to help with your understanding of social learning theory. Bandura, Ross and Ross's (1961) study is outlined on pp. 26–27.

One example of social learning theory in humans

One area where social learning theory is often used as an explanation is the issue of whether children imitate violence that they see on television. There have been examples of behaviour that seem to come directly from television models. For example, young children can be seen to copy pop stars — imitating their clothes and hairstyles, as well as their behaviour. Similarly, young children will imitate the actions of 'heroes'.

Social learning theory explains this by reference to observational learning, which includes modelling and imitation. Children tend to imitate role models of the same sex. Hero figures are often male, so boys are more likely to imitate than girls. Villains, if they are clearly punished, should be imitated less than heroes, because it is more likely that people will imitate those who are rewarded for their actions. However, villains are not always clearly punished, so they may be imitated.

Bandura, Ross and Ross's (1961) study (pp. 26–27) helps to show how children are likely to imitate aggressive behaviour. Studies such as this lend support to social learning theory's claims of how learning takes place. It has been suggested that pro-social behaviour is shown on television too, and is rewarded, so child viewers are more likely to learn moral behaviour. Programmes such as *Sesame Street* have taken up this idea.

The nine o'clock watershed is there to stop unsuitable behaviour being shown on television while children may be watching. This is a practical application of these sorts of ideas, although many do not think there is enough censorship on television. Video games and computer games, as well as internet material, have all also been criticised as modelling unsuitable and aggressive behaviour.

Social learning theory helps to show that children are more likely to exhibit aggressive behaviour if they have the chance to observe it. These issues are addressed below as the problem of showing televised violence is put forward as a contemporary issue. Unit 4 also considers this important issue of television violence and how we learn aggression.

Evaluation

+ Social learning theory is a more complete explanation of learning than either of the other two given here. It incorporates ideas of reinforcement and punishment, as does operant conditioning, but also adds an element of cognition.
+ Behaviourism (classical and operant conditioning) is criticised as being only about external behaviour, and not considering internal factors such as motivation. Social learning theory takes these factors into account.
+ Much of the evidence comes from well-planned laboratory studies, which have been replicated and can be said to be reliable.
− Although developing evidence from laboratory studies can mean it is reliable, it can be argued that validity is sacrificed. For example, a study in which children watch adults hitting a bobo doll, and subsequently hit the doll themselves, might not be measuring aggression — for example, it might be looking at obedience or conformity.
− Genetic elements are not considered. Social learning theory, like other learning theories, focuses on the effects of the environment and does not consider other issues such as genetic/biological causes of behaviour.

AS Psychology

Summary

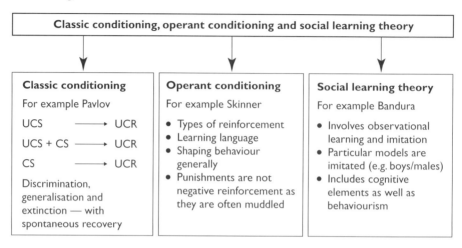

Two studies in detail

Classical conditioning

Watson and Rayner (1920): Little Albert

Aim

This was carried out to explore how classical conditioning could be used to create a phobia where there was none. It aimed to explore how classical conditioning might work with humans, and to look at how emotional responses might be conditioned. Watson and Rayner wanted to try to condition a fear response to something (a pet rat). They wanted to see if this fear response would be generalised to other similar objects. They also looked at how long the response would last, and whether it could it be extinguished.

Method

This was an experiment. Controls were used carefully; an independent variable was manipulated and a dependent variable was measured. It was an experiment done on one person — a single subject design. (This does not make it a case study, however, as case studies gather in-depth data and look at naturally occurring events and actions.)

Procedure

Watson and Rayner chose an 11-month-old baby whose mother worked at the same hospital as them. They chose Little Albert because he seemed very placid and not easily upset. The researchers considered the ethics of the study and it was thought that he would not be too upset.

They established at the start that he was not afraid of rats, rabbits or fur. Then they banged a metal bar behind his head to make a loud noise, and checked that it gave him a startle response, which it did — his lips trembled and he started to cry. They planned to link this startle/fear response to a pet rat that Albert played with.

The researchers banged the metal bar to make a loud noise at the same time as Albert was playing with the rat. Then they tried using other objects such as wooden blocks and fur to see if the fear response was generalised. They made sure the noise was not made when he played with the blocks so he showed no fear then. The researchers left time between the conditioning trials. Then, about 2 months after the original study, they looked to see if Albert was still afraid of the rat, the fur coat and other objects — this was to see if the fear response lasted.

Watson and Rayner had intended to extinguish the fear response but Albert was removed from the hospital before they could do so. However, some reports say that the fear was extinguished.

Results
It did not take many trials (times when they banged the metal bar to make the noise) to lead to a startle response, such as Albert becoming agitated on seeing the rat (without the noise of the bar) and crawling away. When they tried to see what other objects Albert was afraid of (looking for generalisation), they found that he played happily with wooden blocks but showed fear of a rabbit and a fur coat. When they left Albert alone for about 1 month, and checked again to see if he was still afraid of the rat, the rabbit and the fur coat (as well as other things, including a Santa Claus mask) they found that he was.

Conclusion
It was found that an emotional response can be conditioned in an 11-month-old boy. It was found that this response was generalised to other, similar objects. It was also found that the fear response lasted, at least for a little while. They did not explore whether it could be extinguished.

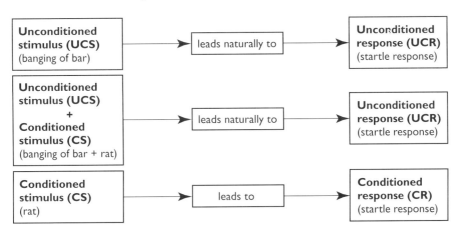

Evaluation

- **+** The study supported Pavlov's findings that dogs learned to associate a laboratory assistant (who brought them food) with food, and so learned to salivate when they saw the laboratory assistant, even without food. The Little Albert study is evidence that classical conditioning is a way of learning.
- **+** There were good controls. For example, the researchers made sure that Little Albert was not afraid of furry things and rats before the study started, so they had a baseline measure. Also, they made sure that they had observable behaviour to measure (such as the startle response).
- **−** This was a study of only one person, so it is hard to generalise and say that these mechanisms apply to everyone (although there is also no reason to say they do not).
- **−** There are ethical issues in that Little Albert learned a fear response, and the researchers frightened him, which goes against ethical guidelines (although these guidelines were not in place at the time). Note also that the researchers did consider this issue, and felt that he would not be harmed.
- **−** The researchers had to repeat the conditioning for it to last. It would seem that it was not easy to condition the fear response.

Observational learning

Bandura, Ross and Ross (1961): the bobo doll study

Note that Bandura did many studies looking at observational learning; this is one of them.

Aim

The study looked at the effects of observational learning. In particular, it dealt with aggression and how children might observe aggressive behaviour and then model their own actions on that aggressive behaviour.

Method

This was a laboratory experiment. It took place in a controlled setting, an independent variable was manipulated and a dependent variable was measured. There was more than one condition, and this means there was more than one IV. It was thought that those who watched aggression would display the most aggression, while those who watched non-aggressive models would display less aggression, as would the control group. It was thought that boys would copy male models more than they would female models, and girls would copy female models more than male models.

Procedure

The dependent variable had to be measurable, so the researchers chose to look at observable aggressive acts. There were 72 children (half were boys and half were girls), all around 4 years old. These children watched either aggressive or non-aggressive models. The children were all from Stanford University nursery school.

There was a control group who did not watch aggressive models at all. The children were all rated for aggression before the study, and the groups were matched to make sure that one did not have more aggressive children in it than another. Both the experimenter and the teacher rated the children, and there was inter-rater reliability.

Eight groups watched various actions, with six children in each group. Of these 48 children, half the groups watched aggressive acts and half watched non-aggressive acts. Some groups watched male models, while some watched female models, which meant that both boys and girls watched both male and female models. The other 24 children acted as the control group and saw neither aggressive nor non-aggressive behaviour.

The children in each of the eight groups were playing in a room when an adult entered. In the 'aggressive' condition, the adult played quietly for a little while in another corner, and then started to behave aggressively towards a bobo doll (the sort you hit and it bounces back). In the non-aggressive condition, the adult continued to play quietly before leaving.

The children were then put into a slightly aggressive state by being told that they could not play with something they found interesting — this was to make sure that all the children were at the same level of aggression themselves, before their behaviour was observed. The group that watched the aggressive acts might otherwise have been less aggressive than the control group, as aggression can have a cathartic effect (it can help to release aggression in the observer). Then all the children were watched playing. They had access to a bobo doll.

Results
The children in the non-aggression conditions showed almost no aggression. Those who watched the aggressive models imitated their behaviour and were aggressive. Children who watched the aggressive models showed both physical and verbal aggression. The aggressive acts observed were clearly those that the adult had carried out; not just general aggression. Those in the non-aggressive condition were the least aggressive (even compared with the control group), so it was thought that watching the non-aggressive model could have had a calming effect. Boys were more physically aggressive than girls but there was little difference with verbal aggression. The aggressive male model seemed to be copied more than the non-aggressive female model.

Conclusion
When children watch adults behaving aggressively, they are likely to imitate that aggression, so it looks as though observational learning takes place. Boys tend to be more physically aggressive. When children watch non-aggressive behaviour they seem to imitate this too, in the sense that it has a calming effect. In general, a male model is imitated more than a female model. It would seem that what we watch affects how we behave.

AS Psychology

> **Evaluation**
> + This study has clear practical applications and has been used to suggest that violence on television can be imitated by children.
> + This is a well-controlled study and is replicable. The researchers deliberately chose behaviour that they could look out for and they recorded baseline measures of aggression (how aggressive the children were at the start).
> - The children were all from one nursery school, so the sample might have been limited in some way. In addition, the study was carried out in the USA, so perhaps results cannot be generalised to other cultures.
> - As this is an experiment, the behaviour is clearly not natural. The children were shown clear aggressive acts and then put in a room with similar toys. Perhaps they thought they were *supposed* to behave in that way towards the bobo doll. This might not have been real aggression, and the findings might not be valid.

Summary

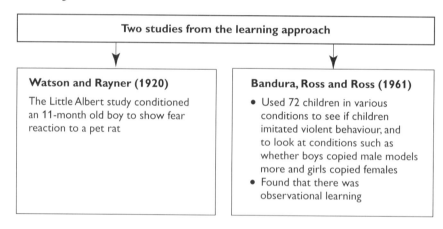

Key application: the deliberate alteration of human behaviour

The mechanisms of classical conditioning, operant conditioning and social learning theory can be used deliberately to change our behaviour. We have seen how we learn through these mechanisms. They can also be used to change what we do, which can be useful in the treatment of problems.

This section considers treatments — that is, deliberately changing a person's behaviour for his/her own good. However, we have to consider who decides what behaviour should be changed and when.

Treatments based on classical conditioning

One example of the use of classical conditioning in humans is systematic desensitisation — it is a treatment for phobias. If you are writing about the key application, outline how systematic desensitisation works (see p. 19).

A phobia can be reduced by using systematic desensitisation. The patient can then live without that fear. This is altering human behaviour deliberately to help someone to overcome a fear.

Evaluation

+ Systematic desensitisation seems to work, so it is a way of changing our behaviour deliberately (it is more effective for small phobias than, for example, for agoraphobia).
+ Systematic desensitisation is intended to help those suffering from a phobia (and does so), so we would say that such behaviour change is good.
+ Phobias are not purely fears, but are fears that affect the sufferers' lives, preventing them from living 'normal' lives. So behaviour change using systematic desensitisation would be helping a person to function 'normally'.
- However, we then need to define what we mean by 'normal'. This will be decided by society, so tends to mean that we expect to obey society's rules. There is the danger that behaviour change by means of conditioning will be undertaken to support a social structure, rather than to aid an individual to function normally.
- Although treating phobias would not be said by many to be conditioning someone to obey social rules (note the emphasis on treatment), there is still the argument that changing someone's behaviour deliberately could be morally wrong.
- When using conditioning principles as treatments, we need to consider who decides that such deliberate alteration of human behaviour is acceptable. Presumably, if the individual is willing to undergo the treatment, that is acceptable. However, there are issues that need to be considered, such as to what extent an individual can make that judgement.

Other treatments based on classical conditioning include alternative treatments for phobias such as 'flooding'. These too can be used as examples of changing human behaviour deliberately.

Treatments based on operant conditioning

Operant conditioning principles can also be used in treatments deliberately to change human behaviour. For example, the token economy programme that is used in mental health institutions and prisons uses operant conditioning principles. Individuals receive tokens when they behave in a desired manner, to encourage them to repeat that behaviour. The tokens can be used by the individuals to buy something they want — they are positive reinforcers. This is a way of replacing maladaptive and undesired behaviour with required or socially desirable behaviour.

AS Psychology

Operant conditioning principles are used in other areas too, such as schools (e.g. giving rewards for good behaviour).

Evaluation

+ The individuals receive praise and rewards for good behaviour, and punishment is avoided, so this treatment can be seen as ethical up to a point.
+ This is a relatively effective way of changing behaviour. It has been shown to work in many areas and it is also reasonably cheap. It can be used in the environment of the individual and no special equipment is needed.
+ People can be trained quite easily to use operant conditioning principles deliberately to change human behaviour.
− Although the use of operant conditioning can be seen as ethical, programmes such as token economy can be criticised as giving power to those administering the system and taking power away from the individual. Such power can be abused; when considering changing human behaviour deliberately, issues such as power are important.
− Programmes such as token economy often take place in institutions and there can be a problem when individuals need to transfer their learning to their own environment.

Summary

Deliberate alteration of human behaviour using principles of learning theories

Classical conditioning principles	Operant conditioning principles
• These have been used in the treatment of phobias; one such treatment is systematic desensitisation • A fear response is replaced by a relaxation response	• These have been used in schools, where good behaviour is rewarded and praised, and bad behaviour ignored • Token economy programmes are another example of the use of operant conditioning — in institutions • TEP may not work outside the institution

Contemporary issue: the effects (especially on children) of violence on television

You can choose a contemporary issue. Here, the issue of whether violence on television is likely to be imitated is chosen because this issue has been outlined already when looking at an example of social learning theory regarding human behaviour.

The issue

Social learning theory can be used to explain how and why children (and adults) copy what they see on television (and other forms of media). In itself, this might not be a problem, and a society might encourage 'good' (prosocial) behaviour in television programmes so that it will be copied. However, the issue is the portrayal of violence and aggression on television. Principles of social learning theory suggest that such violence is likely to be imitated, at least by some people. If violence is portrayed on television, this may lead to violence in society.

Applying concepts from social learning theory

Social learning theory explains how violence on television is likely to be imitated. Refer back to pp. 22–23 where this issue was discussed. Boys are likely to imitate male idols and if these characters are violent and aggressive, boys are likely to repeat the actions they have seen on television. Girls too are likely to imitate females, although we could claim that female characters are less aggressive (in general) on television. The 'bad guys' are not always clearly punished either (at least not soon enough) and a child may not realise that 'good guys' win in the end. The viewer will see the action and the immediate consequence, and associate the two, and violent acts are often portrayed as being successful in the short term. Social learning theory helps us to understand that bad behaviour on television is likely to be imitated, and that models on television have an effect on a child's behaviour. Refer to Bandura et al.'s (1961) study (pp. 26–27) as evidence for the above claims.

It has been suggested that pro-social behaviour is shown on television too, and is rewarded, so child viewers are more likely to learn moral behaviour. Programmes such as *Sesame Street* have taken up this idea.

Summary of the learning approach

- Two key assumptions: the importance of the effect of the environment and a focus on stimulus and response.
- Research methods: laboratory experiments and animal learning studies, including laboratory and field studies.
- In-depth areas of study: mechanisms of classical conditioning, operant conditioning and social learning theory, as well as an example for each of learning in humans, and evaluations.
- Two studies in detail: for example, Watson and Rayner (1920) and Bandura, Ross and Ross (1961).
- Key application: the deliberate alteration of human behaviour, for example treatments or conditioning.
- Contemporary issue: for example, the effect of media violence.

The psychodynamic approach

Two key assumptions

The importance of the unconscious mind

Around nine-tenths of our mind is unconscious, meaning that we cannot access its contents. We cannot access unconscious wishes and desires but they are nevertheless important in motivating our behaviour. We use up energy by repressing unconscious wishes and desires. They are not accessible partly because they are unacceptable — our conscience (superego) will not accept the desires (id). We repress the contents of our unconscious by means of defence mechanisms.

The importance of early experiences

Our personality (made up of the id, the ego and the superego) is formed in the early years (age 0–5 years, approximately). Our experiences in these years can produce problems in the future, depending on how we pass through the first three stages: the oral stage, the anal stage and the phallic stage. If there are problems at any of these stages, we can become fixated at that stage, and this uses energy.

Summary

Two key assumptions of the psychodynamic approach

- Unconscious wishes and desires make up much of our mental processes
- These are kept hidden from us but affect what we do
- We repress them by means of defence mechanisms

- Early childhood experiences (0–5) affect our personality
- During the first three stages, problems can arise — we can become fixated

Research methods used in the psychodynamic approach

Case studies

Case studies are in-depth studies, often of one person. In the psychodynamic approach, case studies involve using many different methods to find out as much about the mental processes of the person as possible, and what environmental influences, especially in early childhood, might have affected their thoughts, wishes and desires. These thoughts, wishes and desires motivate that person to behave and think in certain ways, and if they are inappropriate for that person in some way, a case study might highlight problems and lead to solutions. Case studies are used for research, and also to help individuals move on from any early problems that might be holding them back.

The various methods used include free association, dream analysis, analysis of slips of the tongue, analysis of symbols and clinical interviews. The case study is the overall method, incorporating other methods. Anna O and Little Hans are two case studies from the psychodynamic approach.

Evaluation

+ Real people are studied, so the conclusions drawn have some validity. In-depth data can be gathered.
+ In-depth data are required for a complete analysis of early childhood experiences and to discover what is hidden in the unconscious by means of other methods and interpretations. Other methods, such as experiments, would not be suitable.
+ Although the approach claims that we all follow the same developmental paths in principle (developing id, ego and superego, through oral, anal, phallic, latent and genital stages), in practice we all have different experiences, so each individual must be analysed as such.
− Although case studies are valuable when looking at helping individuals, findings cannot be generalised from one individual's experiences and applied to everyone. Experiments and other methods are used to test some of the assumptions of the approach (such as looking at whether tidiness goes with meanness, for example), and may make findings more generalisable.
− Case studies are not reliable, or at least reliability cannot be tested, as they would be almost impossible to replicate. The same questions and answers are not likely to be used, and the individual would have worked through some problems the first time, and might not be in the same condition again.
− Case studies rely on the interpretation of the researcher; another researcher may not interpret the information in the same way. There is an element of subjectivity in a case study, which can lead to bias.

Clinical interviews

A clinical interview in the psychodynamic approach is when the analyst is listening to the analysand (client). Questions are asked to an extent, but this is not like a structured interview where a set list of questions is asked. It is more like an unstructured interview because the analyst has certain areas that he/she thinks might be of interest, such as early childhood experiences, and will address these areas without using too many direct or prepared questions.

In theory, the analyst does not direct what the client is saying, and just listens. However, in practice, the analyst organises the direction of the flow of ideas and offers explanations. The more the analysand resists the explanation, the more it is tempting to think that the truth is near. However, to an extent, clinical interviews are non-directive, as the analyst wants the analysand to talk enough for unconscious thoughts to be revealed. Clinical interviews gather a great deal of in-depth material about one particular person, and are part of a case study.

Piaget used clinical interviews when conducting investigations in the field of cognitive development (see Unit 1). However, he used the interviews to build a theory without analysis and treatment, and this means his methods differed from Freud's. Piaget too used the method to explore an individual (in this case a child), although he investigated thinking processes, not underlying unconscious wishes and desires. In this way, clinical interviews are used very differently in the two approaches.

Tip

When asked in an examination to outline a research method, think about that method within the relevant approach, as methods are used quite differently. For example, **observations** of animals in a natural setting in the learning approach differ from observations used in the cognitive-developmental approach. Similarly, **case studies** in the cognitive approach to study the effects of brain damage differ from case studies in the psychodynamic approach. **Clinical interviews** are also different in the psychodynamic approach and in the cognitive-developmental approach, as one explores mental health issues, and one explores thinking patterns often by means of experimentation.

Evaluation

+ In-depth material is gathered, which is particularly important in this approach, as the aim is to uncover what is in the unconscious, which is very hard to access.
+ Clinical interviews are part of a case study, and are suited to this approach: the aim is to help the individual, and it is that individual's background, difficulties and thoughts that are to be researched. Qualitative data are required, and clinical interviews (especially as, to an extent, they are non-directive) are a good way of gathering qualitative data.
+ Clinical interviews gather valid data to an extent because the person is listened to without interference (although there may be an element of subjectivity on the part of the analyst).
− There is some direction from the analyst, and the data gathered may, therefore, not be objective because the researcher's own ideas may have affected what was said.
− A clinical interview would be very hard, if not impossible, to replicate, because the material would already have been revealed and discussed, and so the same material is unlikely to be found again in the same form. Clinical interviews could therefore be said to lack reliability.
− It is hard to generalise the findings of one clinical interview to any other situation, and that particular situation is unique. Therefore, as a research method, this form of clinical interview is perhaps only useful for looking at individuals in depth.

Analysis of symbols

Analysis of symbols tends to take place when analysing dreams. However, symbols used in literature and in other situations have also been analysed within this approach.

Dream analysis and dream theory

Dreams are a way into the unconscious. It is very hard to access the unconscious while awake but when we are asleep dream work takes place, and the contents of the unconscious can be interpreted from the content of our dreams. If the contents of our unconscious become conscious, however, we wake up, so to protect our sleep it is thought that the content of our unconscious is revealed by means of symbols.

Symbols might have different meanings to different people (as the contents of each unconscious will be different). However, Freud thought that there are some universal symbols. Many symbols are sexual in nature, as it is likely to be sexual wishes and desires that are repressed in the unconscious.

The manifest content of a dream is what we know we dream about — the content that we reveal when we outline our dreams. The latent content of a dream is the underlying content — what dream analysis can reveal, and what the symbols in the manifest content are hiding. Dream analysis involves listening to the manifest content of dreams and analysing symbols to discover the latent content.

Analysis of symbols in areas other than dreams

Symbols, especially those representing psychodynamic concepts, can be found in other areas, such as literature. This is especially true of the Oedipus complex (see below for an outline of this). For example, in Shakespeare's *Hamlet*, Hamlet delays a long time before avenging his father's death. The psychodynamic approach suggests that young boys (around 5 years old) desire their mother and are jealous of (and want to kill) their father. Hamlet's uncle has murdered his father and married his mother. The young Hamlet, according to the psychodynamic approach, will have wanted to do just that himself. Hamlet's dilemma centres upon his reluctance to kill his uncle and avenge his father's death.

The above is an example of analysis of symbols in literature. The plot is examined to see how unconscious wishes and desires are represented, and this analysis can help to investigate psychodynamic concepts and to illustrate them. Fairy tales too can be analysed and such concepts found. It could therefore be argued that this lends weight to the 'truth' of the concepts.

Evaluation

+ We have dreams that recur frequently; this goes against some other explanations of dreaming, for example that dreams are a random firing of neurones.
+ It is possible to interpret dreams and for the dreamer to accept those explanations. If the interpretation were not plausible, it seems unlikely that an individual would accept the explanation of what the dream symbolises.

- \+ Symbols appear to be repeated in areas such as literature; this adds weight to the idea that these symbols represent some underlying unconscious material.
- − There are explanations for why we dream other than those offered by the psychodynamic approach. These suggest that we dream to organise our thoughts, for example. Alternatively, dreams can be seen as simply a random firing of neurones, and as having no symbolic content at all. These other explanations undermine the psychodynamic claim that dream analysis is useful.
- − When analysing symbols in dreams and elsewhere, there is an element of subjectivity. Symbols need interpretation, which is a subjective activity. Subjectivity is seen as a problem in a research method, as it means that data could be biased rather than true.
- − Writers since Freud will have known about his ideas and may well have incorporated them into their writing, so it is not surprising that literature reveals such concepts.

Summary

Three research methods used in the psychodynamic approach

Analysis of symbols
- Dream analysis involves looking for symbols (often sexual) in the manifest content, so that the latent content can be revealed
- Symbols in literature can be explained using psychodynamic concepts

Case studies
- These are in-depth studies, often of one person
- Studies use many different methods to find out as much about the mental processes of the person as possible
- Early childhood experiences are seen as very important

Clinical interviews
- Interviews gather in-depth material about one particular person, as part of a case study
- They tend to be non-directive as it is important that the individual gives enough information freely for unconscious thoughts to be in some way revealed
- The 'interviewer' (analyst) talks freely, rather than using prepared questions, and thus can gather qualitative data

In-depth areas of study

Freud's theory

You will have learned a lot about Freud's theory by studying research methods commonly used in the approach, so a brief outline is presented here.

Conscious, preconscious and unconscious

Conscious thoughts are those we are aware of. Our everyday behaviour (as far as we are aware) is governed by these conscious thoughts. Preconscious thoughts are those we can become aware of, although at the time we are not aware of them. For example, memories that appear to be forgotten but can be recalled if we focus on them, were in the preconscious. When these memories are focused upon and recalled, they are in the conscious. Unconscious wishes and desires are those we cannot access directly. They influence our decision-making and motivations but we are not aware of them. These unconscious 'thoughts' make up a great deal of our mind (possibly nine-tenths) and have a powerful (but unknown) influence on what we do. We repress these unconscious thoughts and use energy to do so. This makes the theory 'dynamic', as it is active — we are actively trying to protect ourselves from potentially destructive thoughts. We repress these unconscious forces by means of defence mechanisms (outlined below).

Model of personality: id, ego and superego

According to the psychodynamic approach, personality is made up of three 'areas'. These are not separate parts, so much as three different ways of looking at what we are like.

- **Id** is the 'it' of our personality. It represents our wishes and desires — this is the pleasure principle. Biological urges guide us, and as we are usually warm, fed and not thirsty, the psychodynamic approach tends to focus on sexual urges, as they are the ones most likely to be repressed.
- **Ego** is the 'I' of our personality, and represents the reality principle. This is the part of our personality that makes decisions based on the demands of the id and the restrictions from the superego.
- **Superego** is the 'above I' of our personality and includes moral principles and ideas of what we ought to be like. We learn these principles from our parents and upbringing and they tend to go directly against our id's desires. This can be problematic when it comes to making decisions.

Psychosexual stages: oral, anal, phallic, latent, genital

From birth to around 5 years, we move through the first three psychosexual stages according to the psychodynamic approach. There is then a latent stage (during which not much happens) and finally, at puberty, the genital stage. The first three stages are when our personality is formed (id, ego and superego).

The **oral stage** is the first stage (0–2 years), when pleasure is focused on the mouth. The id is in control and the ego and superego have not yet developed, so the baby is demanding. If fixated at the oral stage (having had problems in development), then a person will be passive and dependent and might show such behaviours as smoking.

The **anal stage** is the second stage (2–3 years), where pleasure is focused on the anus. Potty training becomes important. If fixated at the anal stage, a person will tend to have a 'holding back' (anally retentive) character, and show behaviours such as excessive tidiness or meanness. An anally expulsive character is also possible.

The **phallic stage** is the third stage (4–5 years), where a boy develops sexual feelings for his mother, and becomes jealous of his father. The boy thinks his father knows this, and so he fears his father and develops castration anxiety. By hating his father, but by fearing him too, the boy experiences strong emotions. Defence mechanisms come into play to repress these strong unconscious desires; to resolve the problem, the boy identifies with (becomes) his father, so that he can stop hating and fearing him. This is the Oedipus complex. Girls have sexual feelings towards their fathers and identify with their mothers to overcome these. This is the Electra complex, but was not focused on as much as the Oedipus complex for boys. One difference is that boys have castration anxiety, whereas girls have penis envy, which is not as strong an emotion.

The **latent stage** is the fourth stage (5 years to puberty), where boys play with boys and girls play with girls. The superego develops in the phallic stage (where boys and girls are finding out about right and wrong). The latent stage is not the most interesting stage for the development of personality according to this approach. It could be said that not much happens.

The **genital stage** is the final stage (at puberty). What happens here depends on how the individual has worked through the previous stages. If there are no problems or fixations from early childhood, the child develops feelings for the opposite sex. Anxieties reappear though, as the feelings experienced at the Oedipus stage can resurface.

Defence mechanisms

Some examples of defence mechanisms, and examples of the role they play in keeping the unconscious hidden, are outlined below.
- **Repression** is a useful defence mechanism. Threatening unconscious wishes and desires are not made conscious.
- **Displacement** occurs when our urges cannot be recognised for what they are as the ego would not be able to keep the peace between our unconscious urges (id) and society's moral code (superego). Displacement means that feelings are allowed to surface but are focused on something different. For example, aggression that is felt towards a parent can show itself as focused on someone else.
- **Reaction formation** is when strong feelings cannot be allowed to surface in their 'real' form and so surface in reverse form. For example, if someone really hates a brother, but must repress these feelings, then they can show exceptionally strong love for that brother.
- **Rationalisation** is when we carry out a desired (unacceptable) action but give an acceptable reason for it. For example, a father might beat his son and say it is for his own good.
- **Projection** is when the feelings are true (as with rationalisation and displacement) but they are shown towards another person — projected onto someone else.

Dream theory

For information about Freud's dream theory, refer to the research methods section (p. 32). Note that you need to know Freud's dream theory as part of the in-depth material here.

> **Evaluation**
>
> + Freud's theory has been used as a basis for psychoanalysis, which is used as a therapy, so it has practical applications.
> + The theory has been used to develop other areas of psychotherapy, such as modern counselling techniques.
> + It was derived from methods that obtain in-depth qualitative data and allow individuals to talk about themselves — something that is likely to be useful in itself.
> + It has helped to make taboo subjects (for example, those to do with sex) more acceptable in society. This is positive if it means that people are happier, or more balanced in some way, because of it.
> + Some testing of the theory has been done, with some success. Fisher and Greenberg (1977) found that neatness, obstinacy and meanness go together, which lends some support to the idea of anal personality.
> − It is very hard to replicate many of the studies, as they are case studies and the individuals' thought patterns would be changed by the study itself.
> − There needs to be interpretation by an analyst, which leads to subjectivity and likely bias.
> − The theory is hard to test empirically, so it is difficult to gather information to say whether the theory is right or wrong. However, being hard to test does not mean it is wrong.
> − Other studies have not supported Freud's claims. For example, Zigler and Child (1972) found no evidence that the way an infant is fed affects later personality and character.

Erikson's theory

Erikson took Freud's ideas and developed a theory with some differences. He focused more on psychosocial stages than on psychosexual stages, and he also proposed that stages of development continue throughout life rather than stopping after puberty.

Identity

Erikson agreed that early childhood is an important time for development, and also thought that unconscious wishes and desires are of great importance. He agreed that the function of the ego is to balance the conflicting demands of the id and the superego.

For Erikson, the main aim when developing is to establish an identity, and to have a balanced picture of oneself as an individual within a social framework. Unlike Freud, Erikson emphasised cultural aspects of development. He thought that we

AS Psychology

develop according to our genetic structure, but also using a social and cultural context — this is known as the epigenetic pathway. There are eight stages which involve resolving problems arising from our genetic programming and cultural issues. Like Freud, Erikson emphasised the importance of passing through stages successfully, although he did not think problems had to be resolved completely at each stage.

Crises

Each of the eight stages represents a task we have to complete as we progress along the epigenetic pathway (our genetic and biological needs together with cultural forces and issues). These tasks are crises, because they are important and represent conflict. The eight stages (and, therefore, eight conflicts) are outlined below. These are the 'Eight Stages of Man'. Erikson looks at our whole life; his approach is sometimes referred to as a lifespan approach.

Eight stages

Each stage arises from a biological need or an epigenetic principle, in other words, a biological need taking cultural issues into account. (Remember, Freud focused on the biological need, not on cultural aspects.)

(1) Trust vs mistrust — infants learn to trust (or mistrust) those who care for them.
(2) Autonomy vs shame — children gain autonomy and control for themselves (or not).
(3) Initiative vs guilt — children learn to plan their own activities (or not).
(4) Industry vs inferiority — children are either competent or inferior.
(5) Identity vs role confusion — adolescents develop a sense of identity (or not).
(6) Intimacy vs isolation — young adults find an intimate companion (or are lonely).
(7) Generativity vs stagnation — adults are productive at work and have an input into the next generation (or stagnate).
(8) Integrity vs despair — older people see their lives as meaningful (or they despair).

> **Evaluation**
>
> + The stages in Erikson's theory cover the whole lifespan, which seems to be a more appropriate approach than to suggest that development stops at adulthood.
> + The theory is useful precisely because it looks at how adults also go through stages. By looking at the crises that need to be worked through, people can be helped. For example, in adulthood it can be seen that there is a need to feel that one is contributing in some way to the next generation. If that is not the case, it might be the reason for feelings of depression.
> + Erikson thought that the eight stages were like a cycle rather than a list. Those at the beginning of their lives are influenced by others at other stages (for example, babies must have the chance to trust and to develop autonomy, and adults provide that opportunity). This is a strength, as there is an emphasis on interaction.
> − Erikson's theory (like Freud's) is a stage theory and can therefore be undermined if we say that development is continuous.

Edexcel Unit 2

Summary

In-depth areas of study

Freud's theory
- It focuses mainly on unconscious wishes and urges
- Conscious, preconscious and unconscious thoughts
- Model of personality — id, ego and superego
- Defence mechanisms — protect us from unconscious urges
- Dream theory — a way to discover the content of our unconscious

Erikson's theory
- Psychosocial rather than psychosexual
- Eight stages of development
- Looks at lifespan rather than just childhood
- Stages arise from biological needs combined with cultural forces

Two studies in detail

Phobia

The case study of Little Hans, published by Freud in 1909

Aim
This study was carried out by Freud in the course of his research into treating patients with emotional problems (phobias). Freud knew Hans's father, who relayed to him Little Hans's story. The aim was analysis for the purposes of Freud's own research, and also to help Hans with his disruptive dreams and his phobia.

Method
This was a case study, an in-depth study of an individual, gathering a great deal of data using qualitative methods. Usually, a clinical interview would be used, involving such methods as free association and dream analysis. In this case, as a young boy was involved, Freud gathered his data from reports from the father, so this was not exactly a clinical interview; however, dream analysis was used.

Procedure
Hans was a 5-year-old with a phobia. His parents were concerned that he showed anxiety and fear, and they took the problem to Freud, with whom they were acquainted. The procedure was simply to listen to the father's account, ask questions, and apply analysis to certain symbols and instances that Freud thought had particular importance.

Results
Hans's mother seems to have threatened at one stage to cut off Hans's 'widdler' (his penis), and it was thought that this might have caused later problems as anxiety about the threat was buried in Hans's unconscious. It was noted that Hans was interested in animals with 'widdlers' and the fact that his sister did not have one.

Hans had a dream that he wanted a friend of his (a girl) to share his widdling. It was thought that this might have revealed unconscious desires. Hans also dreamed about his bottom. It was thought that he might have gained pleasure from wiping his bottom.

Hans is reported as wanting his father to 'go away', and enjoying the times when his father was away on business. It was thought that this showed his desire to be alone with his mother. Hans's phobia was that a white horse would bite him. It was thought that the horse represented Hans's father, and this showed that Hans was afraid of his father.

Hans was also afraid of falling under the water in the bath. When Freud and the father suggested to Hans that, when his mother was bathing his sister, Hans wished his sister's head would go under the water, Hans agreed that this was the case. It was thought that Hans's fear of water represented his wish to drown his sister. Hans wished both his father and his sister to go away, so he could be alone with his mother.

These are the main findings of the case study — there are further details.

Conclusion
The case study illustrates (among other things) Freud's ideas about the Oedipus complex, where a boy desires his mother sexually and wants his father out of the way, and simultaneously fears his father. It also shows the emphasis on unconscious wishes and urges, and how they can lead to phobias such as the fear of water and of the horse. It could be said that 'everyday' fears can hide unconscious motives.

Evaluation
+ A case study method was appropriate, as in-depth data were required. Measurable quantitative data would not have been appropriate, as the aim was to delve into Hans's wishes, desires and dreams.
+ Psychoanalysis is used to treat phobias and other emotional problems, and arose from case studies such as this one, so a strength of this study is that it led to a useful application.
± As the information is about one individual, and care was taken to explore in great detail, the material should be valid — and to an extent this is the case. However, as Hans's father relayed the information, this validity may be lost.
− Freud himself acknowledged that taking evidence from the father meant that there was likely to be bias. However, he thought that when it appeared that Hans was resisting his father's explanations (relayed to Freud), this was particularly interesting.
− Freud also thought that to understand psychoanalysis, it is necessary to be present when the data are gathered. There is bound to be bias when giving an account of such analysis; it is impossible to give all the details.

- Case studies are in-depth investigations of one person, so it is hard to draw conclusions and then generalise these to the rest of the population. The case of Hans might be unique, and generalising ideas about the Oedipus complex might not be appropriate.

Psychodynamic theory

Dreams in pregnancy, Ablon (1994)

Aim

This is a write-up of a case study, involving the analysis of a pregnant woman. It shows how dreams during pregnancy can be usefully analysed to illustrate psychodynamic concepts. However, the study was not done with this purpose in mind. The aim of the study was to help the client. The case study shows psychoanalysis in action.

Pregnancy seems to take a woman back to her own childhood, and this makes analysis of dreams particularly useful. The analysand (client) was a married architect with low self-esteem, suffering from sadness and anxiety, which is why she was having psychoanalysis. She felt that she was a burden to her parents when she was young. The analysis progressed from before the pregnancy to after the birth.

Method

This was a case study, using clinical interview and, within that, dream analysis.

Procedure

The study was of a 36-year-old woman who had started analysis before she became pregnant, and whose analysis continued throughout pregnancy. It followed standard practice, for example periodic visits of the analysand to the analyst, by appointment, over quite a long period of time. Notes are taken by the analyst, focusing on particular issues, for example the relationship between analyst and analysand, how well appointments are kept, as well as analysis of dreams.

Results

In early pregnancy, the analysand's dreams suggested that she connected having a baby to early bowel movements, which links back to the anal stage. At $3\frac{1}{2}$ months, she dreamt of her father wanting to get into bed and cuddle her. This links to the Oedipus/Electra complex in the phallic stage.

Then she had another dream where the analyst was in bed with her, which is evidence of transference. At 2 weeks after the expected date of the baby, she said she couldn't imagine being a mother, as 'it feels like someone has died'. This seems to mean that she thought that the 'baby' part of her own personality, which longed for appreciation from her mother, had to die for her to become a mother herself.

Conclusion

Pregnancy appears to be a time when dreams are particularly vivid and useful to analyse.

Some themes from analysis of the study and of pregnant women in general include emphasis on changing from girl to mother. For example, in this study the analysand appeared to find it hard to be a mother because she had not sorted out problems in her childhood. Another theme is anxiety at being 'dirty'. Perhaps this reflects early problems in resolving one of the psychosexual stages. This particular analysand feared both injury to herself and being destructive towards her baby. Both these themes occur in other case studies too. These fears could reflect problems in reducing early conflicts too, for example guilt at destructive feelings towards the same sex parent.

Evaluation

+ The findings are supported by other studies carried out during pregnancy, and this strengthens the conclusions.
+ Psychoanalysis allows people to talk about their feelings in a way they may not have done before, so it has a clear application, and the study illustrates this well.
− When interpretation is used, such as in this study, there will almost certainly be bias. The analyst (and the analysand) are looking at certain issues in the client's life, especially early childhood and relationships with her mother and father, so already there is some bias in what is seen as of interest.
− There is a preconception about transference, and the analyst seems to have discussed this with the client, so it may be this discussion that led to the instances where the analysand dreamt of the analyst, rather than 'real' emotions towards him.
− The study cannot be repeated, so it cannot be tested for replicability. It is possible that the results are not reliable, and we cannot test this.

Summary

Two studies from the psychodynamic approach	
Little Hans (1909) • Study of a 5-year-old boy with a phobia of a white horse • It is thought that the horse represents the father and that the case study shows the Oedipus complex	**Ablon (1994)** • Study of a woman during pregnancy and analysis of her vivid dreams • It is thought that in pregnancy there is some reliving of childhood • The study also showed transference

Key application: understanding mental health issues

The main way in which issues arising from the psychodynamic approach are applied is in the field of mental health, most often when looking at mental illness at the point when people need help. However, the approach can also be used to help maintain mental health.

Freud's whole approach focuses on how problems experienced in early childhood can lead to fixation, which then leads to repressed wishes and desires that prevent us leading a problem-free life in adulthood. Erikson's approach, too, focuses on the crises that we need to negotiate successfully in order to move through life steadily without mental health problems, and to arrive in old age in a state of integrity, not despair.

Disorders treated by psychoanalysis include eating disorders, anxiety disorders, personality disorders, sexual dysfunction and depression. The decision as to what treatment would be useful tends to be based on (among other things) the belief about what is causing the problem. Therefore, if a psychodynamic explanation of the causes of a mental illness or difficulty seems useful, psychoanalysis might be seen as a useful treatment for that difficulty.

Evaluation

+ A strength of using the psychodynamic approach to understand mental health issues is that a treatment (psychoanalysis) is then suggested and can be used. Psychoanalysis has been shown to be successful; in our society, we now accept that our early childhood experiences, particularly with parents and siblings, have a strong effect on our later personality. This suggests that the explanations offered by the approach are acceptable.
+ If the problem is caused by underlying repressed emotions, and if these can be brought into consciousness by psychoanalysis, then this is a successful way of understanding mental health issues, dealing with them and perhaps curing them.
− Psychoanalysis can be expensive and time-consuming. It may be that only certain social groups can access psychoanalysis.
− To undergo psychoanalysis, the person needs to have a degree of self-awareness. Not everyone has this self-awareness, either due to their condition or if they are too young. The treatment that is used following the psychodynamic explanation may not help everyone.
− It may be that psychoanalysis leads to a cure. However, it is possible that the treatment helps some of the emotional factors that come from the illness or difficulty without tackling the underlying cause. It may be necessary to look for other causes and treatments at the same time, and denying them to a person may not be fair.

Tip

In Unit 4, the clinical application of psychology looks at some of the areas treated using psychoanalysis (among other treatments and therapies). It would be useful to make links between these two parts of the specification.

AS Psychology

Summary

Understanding mental health issues using the psychodynamic approach

Mental health issues and the psychodynamic approach

- Problems in early childhood can lead to fixation which then leads to repressed wishes and desires
- Erikson focuses on how we can arrive in old age in a state of integrity, not despair
- Disorders treated by psychoanalysis include eating disorders, anxiety, personality disorders, sexual dysfunction and depression
- If a psychodynamic explanation of the cause of a mental illness or difficulty seems useful, psychoanalysis might be seen as a useful treatment for that difficulty

Strengths

- A treatment (psychoanalysis) is suggested and can be used
- Psychoanalysis has been shown to be successful

Weaknesses

- Can be expensive and time-consuming
- The person needs to have a degree of self-awareness

Contemporary issue: false-memory syndrome

You can choose a contemporary issue. Here, the issue of false-memory syndrome is chosen, as it relates well to the key application. You may have studied a different issue.

The issue

Repression is when anything that is a threat to the conscious functioning of the individual is hidden. The aim of psychoanalysis is to release repressed thoughts and desires, so that they can become conscious and be dealt with. Hypnosis and analysis are used to reveal unconscious wishes, desires and experiences from early childhood. The analyst delves into hidden thoughts using hypnosis and other means, and interprets symbols in order to uncover these repressed thoughts. It has been claimed that in doing so, false memories have been 'recalled' — serious issues such as sexual abuse by a father, which never happened. This is known as false-memory syndrome.

Applying concepts from the psychodynamic approach

Usually, the suggestion that such memories are false only occurs later, or at least that was the case until the 'syndrome' was identified. It is likely that a family will be severely traumatised by untrue revelations before false-memory syndrome is suggested.

Psychodynamic principles suggest that something like child abuse would indeed be strongly repressed, and that it would take careful and lengthy interpretation to uncover such serious issues, by means of hypnosis and dream analysis or free association, together with interpretation of symbols. It would not be unusual for problems to be looked for in early childhood and, given the focus on the Oedipus complex (and Electra complex), it would not be unusual, in the case of a female client, to explore the relationship with her father (for example). Given this exploration and its purpose, it can be seen that analysing what is said about the father–daughter relationship might well lead to the idea that abuse has occurred. In some cases this might be true but in other cases the recovered memory may well be false and the idea planted by the analyst (albeit inadvertently).

Summary of the psychodynamic approach

- Two key assumptions: the importance of the unconscious and the importance of early childhood experiences.
- Research methods: case studies, clinical interviews and analysis of symbols.
- In-depth areas of study: Freud's theory and, here, Erikson's theory.
- Two studies in detail: for example, Freud's 'Little Hans' case study and Ablon's study of pregnancy.
- Key application: using the psychodynamic approach to explain mental health issues.
- Contemporary issue: for example, false-memory syndrome.

The physiological approach

Two key assumptions

The importance of genetic influences on behaviour

Genes influence not only the colour of our eyes and hair but also aspects of our behaviour. We inherit 50% of our genetic make-up from our mother and 50% from our father. Temperament, IQ and some illnesses such as alcoholism are all said to have a large genetic factor.

AS Psychology

The importance of the nervous system

Behaviourists claim that our behaviour comes from learning from the environment, but it is clear that between our receiving a stimulus from the environment via our senses and responding to that stimulus, the nervous system must be activated to trigger the response. Cells in the brain respond to various neurotransmitters, and these can lead to different responses. For example, drugs affect the responses of the nervous system at the synapse and different drugs can produce different responses. Our nervous system affects our behaviour.

Summary

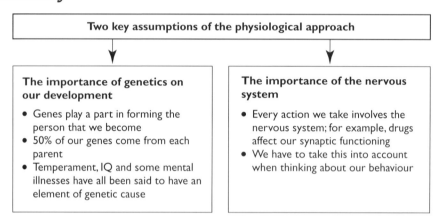

Research methods used in the physiological approach

Brain-scanning, EEG and lesioning

These are all biological methods, although this is a generic term and is not itself a 'method', so don't give it as an answer when asked for a research method within this approach.

Brain-scanning

In CAT (computerised axial tomography) scans, an X-ray moves around the head and images slices of the brain at work. The computer then puts the slices together to form a complete picture. PET (positron emission tomography) scans also involve a computer putting together a picture of the brain from slices, but instead of X-rays, a radioactive tracer is used. This tracer in the body shows up as an area of activity. MRI (magnetic resonance imaging) scans involve a strong magnetic field being passed through the required area of the body. A computer uses the varying responses of different tissues to generate images.

Brain-scanning can be used to try to detect causes of schizophrenia by, for example, comparing the brain activity of identical twins, where one has schizophrenia and the other does not.

> **Evaluation**
> + Scans are accurate.
> + The tests can be replicated and the same results should be found, so the method is reliable.
> ± MRI scans give much clearer pictures than CAT scans.
> − The results rely on accurate analysis by a person, so there is room for error.
> − Scans are expensive (although scanning machines are becoming more common, so this may change) and are in demand for medical use, so their availability for research is limited.

Electroencephalogram (EEG)

This is a non-invasive method, because the brain is not invaded/entered directly. EEG measures electrical activity of the brain. Electrodes are attached to the scalp and activity is recorded and shown on a graph. The EEG is used to measure different levels of consciousness, such as sleep. An EOG (electrooculogram) measures the activity of the eyes, and an EMG (electromyogram) measures muscle activity.

Loomis, Harvey and Hobart (1937) used an EEG to measure sleep patterns.

> **Evaluation**
> + As an EEG is non-invasive, there are few ethical problems with its use, although ethical guidelines must be followed.
> + As an EEG gives scientific measurements and objective data, the method is replicable and therefore reliable.
> − An EEG may change the electrical activity in the brain, so validity can be questioned.
> − Measuring activity does not tell us what causes it, although cause can be inferred. For example, using an EOG we can see that rapid eye movement occurs, and it seems to occur when people dream, but we cannot be sure that the dreams cause the rapid eye movement (or vice versa).

Lesioning, ablations and surgery

These invasive methods study the brain by damaging parts of it or assessing damage that has occurred naturally (e.g. through disease) or by accident. Studies aim to show what behaviours or characteristics are caused by the damage. It is concluded that if damage is done, and certain behaviours occur or are missing, then the damaged area must be responsible for that behaviour (either controlling it or generating it). Animals are used for researching lesions and ablations, as this would not be ethical with humans. However, natural or accidental damage does occur in humans, so they can then be studied too.

Ablation means that an area is removed; lesions are when an area is damaged but not removed.

AS Psychology

Another technique is to stimulate the brain using electrodes, to see what effect that has. An example of stimulating the brain is the study by Bard (1928) when cats were sent into pretend rages. An example of surgery is when Moniz (1935) carried out prefrontal lobotomies to calm aggressive people. Unfortunately, these probably caused more harm than good.

> **Evaluation**
>
> + Using animals, it is possible to target certain areas of the brain so that research can be carried out to see what that area of the brain is for. The studies can be controlled carefully: they are replicable and therefore reliable.
> + There are many similarities between animals and humans, especially in the basic parts of the brain, for example in rats. It is therefore possible to use animals and draw conclusions about humans. Animals breed more quickly and are smaller to handle than humans.
> ± Many would say that using animals presents fewer ethical difficulties, although not everyone agrees with this.
> − Studying animals might seem useful but some people question whether we should generalise the findings from animal studies to humans, or even to other animal species.
> − Brain damage (especially in human studies) is often not limited to one specific area, so it is hard to be sure which part of the brain has what function.

Correlational techniques

A correlation is when two variables covary, which means that one variable changes with the other. When both variables increase together, the correlation is positive. For example, the more time we spend practising, the better we learn a list of words. A negative correlation is when one of the variables increases and the other decreases. For example, the older we are (the more our age increases), the slower we drive (the more our speed of driving decreases). A study with a correlational design usually involves the same person in the two 'conditions', though they are not really conditions. It is just that two things about a person (their age and their driving speed, or the time spent practising and their recall on a word list) vary together. The study, therefore, does not use a matched pairs, independent groups or repeated measures design — this is a correlational design, or a correlation. Correlations are useful for studying genetic influences because there are few direct ways of measuring these. We cannot do an experiment, for example.

Identical (mz, or monozygotic) twins share 100% of their genes. Studies with mz twins are slightly different from the correlational studies outlined above because instead of comparing two variables for one person, the identical twins are compared with one another. A concordance rate is established when a correlational test is carried out comparing how one twin scores on a variable of interest compared with the other twin. For example, IQ is studied in this way. The IQ score for one identical twin can be set against the IQ score for the other identical twin; thus we can see whether one has a high IQ score when the other does too. If this is the case, there would seem to be grounds for saying that IQ is, at least to an extent, genetic in origin.

Family studies and adoption studies are also used. For example, the IQ scores of adopted children can be compared with the IQ scores of their natural mothers and their adopted mothers. This helps to show how much IQ rests upon genes and how much it rests upon environment.

> **Tip**
>
> This issue engages with the nature/nurture debate. It looks at how far a characteristic (in this case IQ) is innate and how far it is affected by environment (learned). You will need to know about the nature/nurture debate for Unit 6.

> **Evaluation**
>
> + Identification of interesting relationships is possible, and these can then be investigated further.
> + With the type of correlations used in the physiological approach, there is often no interference, for example no manipulation of an independent variable, so, to an extent, valid data are found.
> − A correlation only shows a relationship between two variables, and there is no guarantee that the two are linked in any other way. We tend to assume a cause-and-effect relationship (e.g. IQ and genes) but this is not necessarily so.
> − With twin studies, two different people are being compared. Even though they share 100% of their genes, no one is likely to claim that identical twins are identical people. It has been suggested that they have been affected by different environments even before birth.

Summary

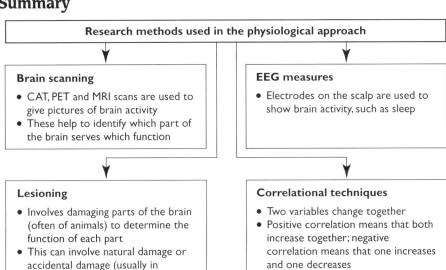

AS Psychology

In-depth areas of study

Circadian rhythms

Circadian rhythms and the day/night cycle

Circadian rhythms are daily cycles, lasting about 24 hours. Examples are temperature, metabolic rate and sleep/wake cycles. All three of these rhythms fluctuate over a 24-hour cycle. The day/night cycle refers to the 24-hour cycle of daylight and darkness that affects us (note that in some countries this cycle is very different from ours). Sleep itself is not a circadian rhythm; within the sleep/wake cycle there are other rhythms that last throughout sleep, for example episodes of REM. Aschoff and Wever (1981) discuss the importance of circadian rhythms for humans. Metabolic rate and temperature, for example, are at their highest in the afternoon, perhaps because we need to be most active then.

Circadian rhythms (and other bodily rhythms) seem to be much the same for everyone. This strongly suggests that they are innate and not learnt.

Endogenous pacemakers and zeitgebers

If circadian rhythms are innate, as they seem to be, then we need to ask whether they are run by an internal mechanism or an external one, and find out what keeps the rhythm going.

Endogenous pacemakers are internal mechanisms. Zeitgebers are external (exogenous) cues from the environment. We seem to use both endogenous pacemakers and zeitgebers to regulate our circadian rhythms. Zeitgebers include daylight, sunshine, triggers for when we should eat and even television programmes. Siffre (1972) spent 7 months in a cave with no zeitgebers to see what effect it would have on his circadian rhythms. He settled to around a 25-hour cycle. This comprised a number of different rhythms (temperature, sleep and so on). The Siffre study shows that we have a 25-hour cycle and yet we work to a 24-hour day, so zeitgebers must have a role in controlling our rhythms. The main endogenous (internal) pacemaker is the body clock, in the suprachiasmatic nucleus (SCN — a physical part of the brain). Evidence for this is that if the SCN is damaged, circadian rhythms become random over the day. The retina in the eye responds to light, and this affects the SCN, so this is the link between zeitgebers and the body clock. It is the 24-hour day/night cycle that governs our circadian rhythms. It seems that we can reset our body clocks, for example if we do shiftwork or fly halfway around the world. Some people can reset their clocks better than others, so endogenous pacemakers must vary between people.

> **Evaluation**
>
> + Studies done on animals confirm the evidence for circadian rhythms, and triggers being both internal and external. Certain areas of the brain are damaged or removed to see the effect, and findings show that with no SCN, for example, rhythms are affected.

- + Studies such as Siffre's are experiments and are well controlled, so seem to give reliable data.
- + Tests reinforce the findings. For example, keeping a temperature chart can show that temperature fluctuates over a 24-hour period.
- ± Some studies of sleep deprivation reinforce the idea that we need sleep, and suggest that we need circadian rhythms to function. However, there are studies that show that sleep deprivation for some people has a different, less serious, effect (e.g. Dement, 1972). So there is some contradictory evidence.
- − Individual differences are found. Some people do not experience jet lag, for example. This suggests circadian rhythms are more complex than a single mechanism that guides us all in the same way.

Stages of sleep and EEG criteria

Sleep is an ultradian rhythm, which is one that lasts less than a day. The sleep/wake cycle is a circadian rhythm but sleep itself is not. The main sleep pattern (not when taking naps) comprises around five cycles each night. Each cycle is divided into five stages. Aserinsky (1952) used an EOG to measure eye movements and found that rapid eye movement (REM) occurred more than once during the night and seemed to be part of a number of sleep stages. Dement and Kleitman (1957) woke people when they observed rapid eye movement and discovered that more 'real' dreams were reported than when they woke people at other times. EEG patterns show that there are different stages of sleep, with the brain showing varying activity levels. There are four stages of non-REM (NREM) sleep; the fifth stage is REM sleep.

Evaluation

- + Sufficient studies have looked at sleep and dreaming to conclude that there are different patterns of brain activity at different times during sleep, and that there is a cycle which is repeated throughout the night.
- + EEG measures are objective and seem easy to interpret, so evidence is reliable.
- − We do dream in NREM sleep too, although perhaps not as vividly.
- − Waking people up to ask them what they remember is not a very reliable method. They will be confused, and there is no way to test that what they report is truthful. They may not find it easy to say what they were 'thinking' of if they are woken in that way.

Theories of sleep: evolutionary and restoration theory

Theories of sleep look at the functions that sleep performs.

Evolutionary theory

Meddis (1979) suggests that we have evolved our sleep patterns — in other words, we sleep because it enhances our chances of survival. Sleeping must have been useful for our survival at one time. This is the evolutionary theory of sleep; it claims that there is survival of the fittest, which means that whatever characteristics we have are there because they are or were once useful.

This is backed by other research. For example, it has been shown that animals that were at risk from predators did not sleep much, presumably so that they could remain aware. Cows napped (and still do) for 2 hours at a time, for example. Animals that can sleep safely hidden away are more likely to sleep for 14 hours. These examples suggest that sleep patterns evolve to suit the situation, and lead to the most likely chance of survival.

> **Evaluation**
>
> + Saying that sleep is useful seems to be a sensible explanation, and fits in with evolutionary explanations of other characteristics, e.g. giraffes having a long neck to reach leaves on high branches. The idea of survival of the fittest is widely accepted.
> − Other theories suggest that there are more positive reasons for sleeping, such as restoring ourselves. It could be that sleep has (or had) the function of helping us to survive, as well as restoring certain physiological processes.

Restoration theory

The restoration theory gives sleep a more active role, and a more positive reason for its existence than just helping us to survive. Oswald (1966) claims that our bodies can repair cells and restore energy while we sleep. It is possible, too, that our neurotransmitters are restored while we sleep.

During sleep, the pituitary gland releases a hormone that is used in tissue growth, and this suggests that there is restoration while we sleep. Furthermore, as we get older we sleep less, which could be taken to mean that, as we become less active, we need less restoration.

> **Evaluation**
>
> + Evidence shows that when we do more physical activity we sleep more, and this supports the theory that we need restoration.
> + This area is not easy to research, although studies showing hormone release do give evidence for the theory.
> − Taking more exercise makes us sleep more but less exercise does not make us sleep less, so this is not evidence for restoration theory, unless there is a minimum amount of sleep that we need.
> − There is a lack of precise evidence to show that we need sleep to restore ourselves biologically.

One physiological theory of dreaming

The activation–synthesis model: a physiological explanation of dreaming

Hobson and McCarley (1977) suggest that during sleep, parts of the brain are active and to make sense of this, a story is built up which takes the form of a dream. It is suggested that during REM, the brain is ready to make sense of stimuli but there are no external stimuli, so the brain uses memories and starts making sense of these. Studies with cats (Hobson, 1989) suggest that there is firing of neurones in the brain during sleep. Cells involved in vision and walking can be activated, but as the body is not moving (in REM sleep the body is paralysed) this activation is synthesised (made sense of) and that synthesis becomes a dream.

> **Evaluation**
> + Dreams do not make perfect sense and this fits with the activation–synthesis model, which suggests that dreams are our interpretation of random firing of neurones.
> − Dreams are often meaningful and even seem to use information from previous events. The activation–synthesis model does not predict meaningful dreams, at least not dreams that use information we know about, such as last night's film.
> − People have recurring dreams and dreams that seem to be personally meaningful. This is not explained by the activation–synthesis model.

Summary

Circadian rhythms, two theories of sleep and one physiological theory of dreaming		
Circadan rhythms • Last over 24 hours • External cues called zeitgebers trigger our rhythms • Internal cues called endogenous pacemakers, as well as our body clock, keep the rhythms going • Some people adjust their rhythms better than others	**Restoration theory of sleep and evolutionary theory** • Evolutionary theory suggests that we sleep to avoid predators (or did some time ago) and that sleep has a survival value • Restoration theory suggests that during sleep, certain physiological aspects of the body (e.g. hormones for growth) or cells are restored	**One physiological theory of dreaming** • The activation–synthesis model: Hobson and McCarley (1977) • Random firing of neurones in the brain during REM sleep are interpreted by the brain into a story (a dream)

Two studies in detail

REM sleep

Dement and Kleitman (1957)

Aim
Dement and Kleitman looked at REM sleep for a number of reasons. They wanted to see whether dreams are found more in REM than in NREM sleep. They wanted to see if the length of REM had any link to the length of the dream, and if the REM pattern represented the content of the dream in any way.

Method
This was a laboratory study using an EEG to measure brain waves. Eye movements were also measured. There was no manipulated independent variable, so it was not an experiment. It was not an in-depth study, so it was not a case study. Observations were carried out, and participants were interviewed and asked about their dreams. There were controls and the setting was artificial, so this was a laboratory study using observation and interview.

Procedure
Seven males and two females were the participants in the study. Most of the data came from five of these participants. Participants were allowed to sleep and their brain activity was measured using an EEG. The researchers watched eye movements and recorded their direction and the time they lasted for. They also asked participants questions about their dreams. The experimenter was not there when the dreams were recalled, so that experimenter effects were controlled for. Participants ate normally all day but did not drink alcohol or take caffeine. They arrived before bedtime and electrodes were fitted for the EEG measures. During the night, participants were woken up and asked about their dreams. Then they went back to sleep. In each 2-hour period (over the course of 8 hours), the researchers noted how often they woke the participants — in other words, how often they observed REM sleep. In each 2-hour period they woke the participants on average 23% of the time. This means that the interruptions were spread throughout the night fairly evenly, and that for around a quarter of the time there was REM sleep.

Results
All the participants had periods of REM, which became longer as sleep progressed, varying from 3 to 50 minutes. REM sleep produced more dreams than NREM sleep. On being woken, one of the questions was how long the participants thought they had been dreaming. They found this hard to do, so they were woken when 5 or 15 minutes into the dream and then asked whether they thought they had been dreaming for 5 or 15 minutes. They could do this. The longer the REM sleep, the more they could recall of their dream. There is some evidence to link actual eye movements (e.g. vertical) with dream content.

Conclusions
Dreaming seems to occur in REM sleep, and there are REM periods throughout the night. The study suggests that everyone dreams, even if they do not recall their dreams. Physical eye movements in REM seem to reflect the content of the dream (or vice versa).

> **Evaluation**
>
> + Good controls mean that the study is replicable and reliable, in that the procedures can easily be repeated. Some of the measures were quite objective, such as observing when REM happens and watching the actual movements of the eye.
> + The activation–synthesis model of dreaming claims that our brains are active during

REM sleep and this supports the idea that we dream in REM sleep. The study's findings are backed by other evidence and theories.
- Not many participants were used. This is possibly a strength from an ethical viewpoint but means that it is hard to generalise the findings to the rest of the population.
- Self-reports were used when participants reported the content of their dreams; these are often subjective, so not reliable.
- Dreams were reported in NREM too. It is possible that there is just as much intense dreaming in NREM but the dreams are less well recalled.

Sleep deprivation

Rechtschaffen et al. (1983)

Aim

The researchers wanted to see the effects of sleep deprivation; their aim was to look for the reasons for why we sleep.

Method

This was a controlled laboratory experiment using rats, which have similar brain structures to humans. There was an experimental group, which was deprived of sleep, and a control group, which was not. The IV was whether the rats were kept awake or not, and the DV was what happened to each rat, measured by whether or not they died.

Procedure

The researchers set up apparatus. The rats were placed on a disc that was partly submerged in a bucket of water. EEG patterns showed when the rat fell asleep and as soon as that happened, the disc started to rotate. If the rat did not walk on the disc as it turned, it would fall off into the water. This device kept the rat awake. Another rat was placed on another disc set up in the same way except that when this rat (the control) fell asleep (as shown by EEG patterns) the disc did not rotate, so the rat could stay asleep. More than one pair of rats was used.

Results

After 33 days of the above treatment, all the rats that had been deprived of sleep died. None of the control rats died.

Conclusion

Sleep seems to be very important for us to survive. It is not clear exactly why the rats died. The researchers thought it was because they were unable to regulate their body temperature, but this was not confirmed.

Evaluation

+ The careful controls mean that the study is replicable — in fact, the researchers did replicate it and used more than one pair of rats. Therefore, the findings are reliable.

- Many ethical issues are dealt with by using animals rather than humans, but others remain important.
- Using animals and then generalising the findings to humans is considered by some to be unjustified because of differences between humans and animals.
- Horne (1988) pointed out that not only were the rats deprived of sleep but they were also stimulated by having to walk, which could have been a confounding variable and contributed to the results.

Summary

```
                Two studies from the physiological approach
                        │                        │
                        ▼                        ▼
```

Dement and Kleitman (1957)	Rechtschaffen et al. (1983)
• Aimed to confirm that most dreams take place in REM sleep • Looked at eye movements to see if they reflect the dream content, and studied the length of REM/recall of dream	• Rats were placed on a disc partly submerged in water • One rat was placed on the disc and an EEG monitored brain patterns • When these showed that the rat had fallen asleep, the disc rotated and the rat had to walk to keep out of the water • Thus the rat was kept awake • A control rat was allowed to sleep • The rats that were kept awake died

Key application: circadian rhythms, shiftwork and jet lag

Shiftwork

Studies into circadian rhythms suggest that we need to sleep. Although research suggests that we can adapt to different rhythms, this is not easy and some people adapt more easily than others.

Shiftwork means that we have to adapt frequently to changes in our sleep/wake cycle and research suggests that this is not an easy thing to do; it can have consequences such as illness. Shiftworkers seem to suffer from digestive problems and are often tired and irritable — this supports the idea that changing our daily rhythms can be harmful. Disasters such as Three Mile Island and Chernobyl have been blamed on problems with workers trying to stay awake and concentrate in the early hours of the morning.

Research by Czeisler et al. (1982) suggests that shifts can be rotated but this should be forwards so that workers move from day to evening shift, then from evening to night shift, then from night to day shift. Each shift should last for at least 18 days so that adjustment can occur.

In shiftwork, the wrong zeitgebers occur (it is dark outside, for example). Using artificial zeitgebers would improve the chances of adapting to shift changes. One of the problems with shiftwork is that some rhythms adjust more quickly than others. For example, body temperature is slow to adjust. So the person experiences internal rhythms that do not correspond with their activity levels.

> **Evaluation**
> + The study of shiftwork is useful as it has a practical application. Workers can be helped to adjust to shiftwork patterns and employers can achieve better productivity and a happier, more stable workforce.
> − There are problems with studying shiftwork. Employees may be concerned about comments getting back to employers.

Jet lag

Air travel means that we may take off from one time zone and land in another. We then have to adjust immediately to a different time of day. Our circadian rhythms expect one time of day whilst the body is faced with the demands of a different time of day. Physiological problems that result are called jet lag. With other methods of travel, for example by sea, an individual would adjust gradually.

Symptoms of jet lag include poor concentration, inability to sleep at night, loss of appetite and headaches. It is not the length of the flight that causes the problems, as jet lag is not experienced if you fly north or south within the same time zone. Moreover, if the different customs and social setting were the cause of the symptoms, then we would not get them when we fly back home, yet we do. Jet lag is worse when you fly east, because it is harder to advance the body clock (you are in an earlier time zone) than to delay it (which is needed when you fly west). Jet lag can be avoided to an extent if you adapt immediately to the zeitgebers in the new time zone. If it is dark and time for sleep in that time zone, then go to bed. If it is daylight, then stay up.

> **Evaluation**
> + As with shiftwork, the study of jet lag and circadian rhythms has useful practical applications. Pilots and others working in the air travel industry need to know how to overcome the symptoms of jet lag, as do all travellers.
> − There are ideas linking diet with jet lag but more research is needed in this area.
> − Melatonin appears to help the body clock to adjust, but it is not clear how.
> − There are many factors involved in jet lag; some might be psychological, to do with arriving in a strange country, or to do with knowledge of jet lag itself.

Summary

Key application of the physiological approach

Shiftwork
- Shiftworkers need help to adjust to different shift patterns
- Research shows that moving a worker forward through shifts helps, and that a worker should not change shifts weekly
- Serious incidents like Chernobyl have been blamed on shiftworkers working in the early hours of the morning and making mistakes

Jet lag
- Symptoms of jet leg are experienced when people fly from one time zone to another and do not have time to adjust
- It is worse when flying east, as it is harder to advance a body clock than to delay it
- Adjusting immediately to zeitgebers in the new time zone can help

Contemporary issue: the 24-hour society

You can choose a contemporary issue. Here, the issue of a 24-hour society is chosen, as it relates well to what has been said above. You may have learnt a different issue.

The issue

The demands of our society mean that more shops and businesses are open 24 hours a day and 7 days a week — a 24/7 society. Hospitals and other services have been staffed for 24 hours a day for many years. It seems from research that we have a number of circadian rhythms that fluctuate fairly regularly over a 24-hour cycle. We can adapt to changes, but not easily and not if the changes happen often. Shiftwork arising from a 24-hour society could affect the health of workers.

Applying concepts from the physiological approach

Circadian rhythms are those that fluctuate over a 24-hour cycle. We use zeitgebers (external cues), for example daylight and meal times, to regulate these rhythms. If we work during the night when it is dark, and try to sleep during the day when it is light, then we are going against the training of our circadian rhythms. Some rhythms adapt more quickly than others, so we might feel alert enough when we work at night but our temperature body clock might not have adjusted. These sorts of disruptions can cause illnesses. Research suggests that we should not change shifts every week, because this does not give us time to adjust. We should move forward through shifts, from day to evening, evening to night, and night to day, rather than backwards. Some people are more suited to the demands of adjusting to shiftwork than others.

Summary of the physiological approach

- Two key assumptions: the influence of genes on behaviour and the importance of the nervous system.
- Research methods: brain-scanning, EEG and lesioning, as well as correlational techniques to look at genetic influences.
- In-depth areas of study: circadian rhythms including endogenous pacemakers, zeitgebers, day/night cycle, EEG patterns and sleep; restoration and evolutionary theories of sleep; one physiological theory of dreaming (activation–synthesis).
- Two studies in detail: for example, Dement and Kleitman (1957) and Rechtschaffen et al. (1983).
- Key application: circadian rhythms and the effects on shiftwork and jet lag.
- Contemporary issue: for example, the 24-hour society.

Questions & Answers

The questions that follow are presented in three sections, one for each of the approaches.

Choose one approach and revise the material using this unit guide. Work through the questions for your chosen approach, answering them yourself without reading the advice on how to answer the question and without reading the answer given. Then mark your own answers, and read through the advice on what is required. Did you interpret the question successfully? Read through the answers given and note where the marks are awarded. Finally, read through the examiner's comments to see what a full answer should include.

Once you have prepared answers for all the questions in a particular approach, answer them again but this time choose a different topic. For example, if you answered a question on a key assumption, then answer it again using the other assumption that you have prepared. If you have described a study within the approach, then describe your other chosen study. If the question is about one in-depth area (e.g. classical conditioning), then answer it as if it were about the other in-depth area (e.g. operant conditioning).

Examiner's comments
All questions and answers are followed by examiner's comments. These are preceded by the icon ℮. They indicate where credit is due and point out areas for improvement, specific problems and common errors such as poor time management, lack of clarity, weak or non-existent development, irrelevance, misinterpretation of the question and mistaken meanings of terms.

Section 1

The learning approach

Key assumptions

(1) Outline *one* key assumption of the learning approach. (3 marks, AO1)
(2) Give *two* key assumptions of the learning approach. (2 marks, AO1)
(3) In the boxes below, tick the *two* statements that apply to the learning approach. (2 marks, AO1)

- We develop through childhood through a series of stages, which are particularly important up to the age of 5 ☐
- We develop through interactions with our environment; we experience stimuli and learn responses ☐
- Our genetic make-up has a great influence on our development ☐
- Behaviour can be measured objectively ☐

e **(1)** Say three things about a key assumption of this approach. 1 mark is likely to be for knowing the assumption (naming it), and 2 further marks for saying more about it. An example is a useful idea, but keep it short as it will not be worth 2 marks.

(2) Just naming two key assumptions is fine. You don't have to say more about them.

(3) Two ticks are required — no crosses. Put a tick against each of two statements that you think are correct.

Answers to key assumptions questions

(1) Environment is important and what happens to us shapes our learning. ✓

e This is fine for 1 mark, but needs more detail, perhaps about observational learning, or about how we respond to stimuli.

(2) Learning is continuous throughout our lifetime, as our behaviour is shaped by continual interaction with environmental influences. ✓ Our environment shapes us, and genetic influences are not considered. ✓

e The two assumptions are clearly given here — in fact, the marks would be given for less detail than this.

(3)
- We develop through childhood through a series of stages, which are particularly important up to the age of 5 ☐
- We develop through interactions with our environment; we experience stimuli and learn responses ☑ ✓
- Our genetic make-up has a great influence on our development ☐
- Behaviour can be measured objectively ☑ ✓

e This is correct, for 2 marks.

AS Psychology

section 1

Common research methods

(4) Give *one* strength and *one* weakness of animal experiments as a research method. (4 marks, AO2)
(5) Describe *one* research method commonly used in the learning approach. (4 marks, AO1)

> **e** (4) There are two things to do and 4 marks available, in this case 2 marks for the strength and 2 for the weakness. Don't just give an answer for each: be sure to expand it enough for the full 2 marks. For example, say what the strength is and then add more detail to explain it further.
>
> (5) 1 mark can be gained by naming or talking about a suitable research method. 3 further marks are available for describing the method. Remember that each point must be descriptive and not evaluative. For example, say that a laboratory study takes place in a setting that is unnatural for the participant, but do not say (for this question) that a laboratory study is not valid.

Answers to common research methods questions

(4) Animal experiments can be said to be unethical, as animals are often harmed and cannot give consent. ✓ A strength is that such experiments can be controlled better than when using humans, as animals are easier to handle and new learning experiences, such as finding the way out of a maze, can be set up. ✓✓

> **e** The weakness is quite well outlined but more needs to be said about ethical issues as this answer is rather vague. The strength is clearer and worth 2 marks.

(5) Laboratory experiments are used ✓ and variables can be controlled very well. ✓ The experimenter gives a participant a task to do where quantitative data will be obtained. ✓ Experiments can be generalised.

> **e** Marks are awarded for naming the method (laboratory experiment), for saying that variables are well controlled, and for mentioning that quantitative data are obtained. However, the method is not described well. Marks could be obtained by talking about manipulating an IV to measure a DV, or discussing different types of design.

■ ■ ■

In-depth areas of study

(6) Describe *two* mechanisms of classical conditioning. (4 marks, AO1)
(7) Outline *one* example of social learning in humans. (3 marks, AO1)
(8) Evaluate operant conditioning as an explanation of human behaviour. (5 marks, AO2)
(9) From the following six terms, tick the two that apply to classical conditioning: (2 marks, AO1)

Unconditioned stimulus	☐	Punishment	☐
Positive reinforcement	☐	Observational learning	☐
Modelling	☐	Discrimination	☐

Edexcel Unit 2

e (6) There are two tasks to do and 4 marks available, so 2 marks for each. 1 mark is given for each mechanism, and in each case a further mark can be given for saying more about it.

(7) 1 mark is given for the example itself and 2 further marks are for elaboration — linking concepts from the social learning approach to the example, and saying how it is an example of social learning in humans.

(8) There are 5 marks for evaluation. One way of getting the marks is to give five different evaluative points; another is to give two or three evaluative points and expand on each. When evaluating, consider what operant conditioning does and does not explain well. Consider too how it does not take into account an alternative explanation. There are other points that you could give.

(9) Two ticks only are required — no crosses.

Answers to in-depth areas of study questions

(6) Classical conditioning involves generalisation. This is when a response has been conditioned, for example salivating when a bell is rung, and then that response also occurring when a different tone of bell is rung. ✓✓

e There is nothing wrong with the description of the first mechanism but there is no second mechanism, so only 2 marks are awarded. Other mechanisms that could be outlined include discrimination and extinction.

(7) A baby might learn to feed itself by watching its mother put her spoon in her mouth. ✓ The baby watches others eat and imitates their behaviour. ✓

e 1 mark is given for the example and another mark for showing how this is social learning and involves imitation. 'Watching' is almost worth another mark, but needs more elaboration.

(8) Operant conditioning has been used successfully to explain issues such as how babies learn language. ✓ However, there are criticisms; for example, young children use words such as 'sheepies' which will not have been reinforced. It seems that we might have an innate device for learning language, so operant conditioning can explain language learning to an extent but not completely. ✓✓ Operant conditioning has been used successfully in schools to reward good behaviour and this adds weight to it as an explanation of human behaviour. ✓ Similarly, token economy programmes work on operant conditioning principles and are successful. ✓

e This is a good answer, gaining full marks. It focuses on how operant conditioning is used, and how its success is evidence for the explanation being useful and probably right. Another way of answering the question is to look at how evidence for operant conditioning mechanisms is gained — using animal studies, for example. Criticising the use of animals in studies and saying, for example, that we cannot generalise to humans, is a way of evaluating.

AS Psychology

(9) Unconditioned stimulus ✔   Punishment ☐
Positive reinforcement ☐   Observational learning ☐
Modelling ☐   Discrimination ✔

e Classical conditioning involves an unconditioned stimulus and discrimination but none of the other terms. Operant conditioning also involves discrimination but that does not matter for this question.

■ ■ ■

Two studies

(10) Describe *one* study from the learning approach. (5 marks, AO1)
(11) Evaluate *one* study from the learning approach. (5 marks, AO2)
(12) Discuss *one* study from the learning approach. (10 marks, essay)

e **(10)** Note that just describing what was done in the study (the procedure) or what was found (the results or findings) is not enough for all 5 marks. For the first mark, make sure the study is identifiable. A further mark can be gained by saying why the study was done. 2 marks can be gained by saying what was done, and 2 more by saying what was found (the results). Marks can also be gained by giving the conclusion. There are more ways than one to get the 5 marks. Be sure to write enough, as for 5 marks you are trying to say five things.

(11) Evaluation can come in many forms. You can give ethical issues (good and/or bad), alternative theories or studies, methodological problems (such as the reliability of experiments or the limitations of case studies), or criticisms of the study itself. Make sure you write enough for 5 marks. You are trying to say five things, although it is possible to gain more than 1 mark for a good, well made point.

(12) This is an essay question. 2 marks are for clarity and communication, gained by correct use of terms, good spelling and avoiding note form. 2 marks are for balance and breadth, gained by giving a good balance of AO1 (knowledge and understanding) and AO2 (evaluation and comment). This leaves 3 AO1 marks and 3 AO2 marks. You need to say three clear things about the study, and make three clear points in evaluation. You can use the same material as in (10) and (11) above. Use some linking words, though, to form a discussion.

Answers to two studies questions

(10) Pavlov taught dogs to salivate by means of classical conditioning. ✔ A neutral stimulus is associated with a response. For example, an unconditioned stimulus leads to an unconditioned response. ✔ Then an unconditioned stimulus (food) plus a conditioned stimulus (bell) leads to an unconditioned response (salivation).

Finally, the bell will give salivation. ✓ This method can help people to overcome a phobia.

e 1 mark is given for the study; Pavlov's is a suitable choice. 2 more marks are given for outlining the basic points about classical conditioning and indicating that Pavlov paired food with a bell to produce eventually salivation to the bell alone. However, this is not expressed very well, and the study itself is not clearly described. Findings are given by saying that the bell gave salivation, and there is some hint as to what was done (pairing the bell and food) but it is by no means clear. More descriptive points are needed for full marks. The sentence about overcoming phobias could have been part of a conclusion but was not a conclusion of Pavlov's study, and so gains no marks.

(11) In Bandura's study, children observed an adult hitting a bobo doll. The children were then watched and their aggression was measured. The study can be criticised as being unnatural. This was an experiment in controlled conditions, so it could be said to show unnatural behaviour, which means the findings are not valid. ✓✓ Similarly, the situation itself was unnatural, as children do not usually observe adults carrying out specific aggressive acts (in this case against a bobo doll) and then get put in a position where they have the opportunity to do the same (a bobo doll is in the room with them). ✓ The children may have thought they ought to hit the doll in that way ✓ — they may have been showing obedience as much as aggression. ✓

e Two main points are made here. The first is that the method is unnatural, so the findings are not valid. The second point is that the set-up is also unnatural. Although these are similar points, the candidate says enough for full marks. Just saying that the controlled conditions made it unnatural gets 1 mark; the second mark is for mentioning validity. Making the point about the situation being unnatural gets another mark, and then a further mark is awarded for elaborating, and saying that the study was set up in a way that might even encourage the behaviour that was found. Finally, a mark is given for further elaboration, in saying that obedience might have been what was found, not aggression. There are other ways of evaluating this study, for example considering ethical issues.

(12) Bandura, Ross and Ross (1961) carried out a study where children were put into different conditions to see if they would imitate adult behaviour. ✓ (AO1) Some children watched an adult behaving aggressively towards a bobo doll, and some watched non-aggressive behaviour. Sometimes the adult was male and sometimes female. ✓ (AO1) There was also a control group, in which the children watched neither aggressive nor non-aggressive behaviour. It was found that children who watched an adult hitting a bobo doll were more likely to imitate that behaviour and to hit the doll too. ✓ (AO1) It was concluded that children imitate aggression and might copy violence on television. The problem with this study is that the children, having watched an adult hitting a bobo doll, may well have believed that they had to do the same thing. This is especially likely as a bobo doll

AS Psychology

was in the room when they went to play. They would be showing obedience, not aggression. ✓✓ (AO2) Also, this is a controlled experiment which is in any case likely to yield conclusions that are not valid, due to the unnatural conditions. ✓ (AO2) We could also say that an American study such as this one may not be useful when looking at the effects of children modelling aggression on adults in another different culture. Yet it is generalised. **(Maximum AO2 marks have already been achieved.)**

> There are more than 10 points here, but when maximum marks are achieved, no more are noted. This answer describes a study clearly and then evaluates it, which is what is asked for. The study is suitable, and there is good balance between description and evaluation. 2 balance and breadth marks are given and 2 communication marks, giving full marks.

■ ■ ■

Key application

(13) Discuss how concepts from learning theory have been used in the deliberate alteration of human behaviour. (10 marks, essay)

> **(13)** This is an essay question. 2 marks are for clarity and communication, gained by use of correct terms, good spelling and avoiding note form. 2 marks are for balance and breadth, gained by giving a good balance of AO1 (knowledge and understanding) and AO2 (evaluation and comment). This leaves 3 AO1 marks and 3 AO2 marks. You need to say three clear things about how learning theory has been used to alter human behaviour deliberately and make three clear points in evaluation.

Answer to key application question

(13) Many treatments are based on learning theory. For example, psychoanalysis is used to listen to people talk about their dreams or thoughts and then analyse what is said to try to help them. Token economy programmes are used in institutions. Patients are given tokens when they show desired behaviour ✓ (AO1) and then save up these tokens to buy something they want. ✓ (AO1) The tokens are positive reinforcement and the idea is that this will make the person repeat the behaviour.

> The first part of this answer refers to psychodynamic theory, and so is ignored. The candidate then talks about TEPs, but only considers one concept — positive reinforcement. This answer gets only 2 of the AO1 marks, as another concept should be considered for the third mark. There is no evaluative comment, so no AO2 marks can be awarded. Terms are used quite well up to a point but are used wrongly when psychoanalysis is considered, and are also limited, so only 1 mark is awarded for clarity and communication. Balance is poor as only one idea is given, so just 1 mark is given for balance and breadth, making a total of 4 marks.

Edexcel Unit 2

Contemporary issue

(14) Outline *one* contemporary issue or debate that can be explained using the learning approach. (3 marks, AO1)

(15) Explain how the learning approach can help us to understand this issue or debate. (6 marks, AO2)

(16) Use your knowledge of the learning approach in psychology to describe and explain *one* contemporary issue or debate. (12 marks, essay)

> **(14)** You need to describe the issue briefly here. Try to avoid applying theories if you can. Some issues are hard to separate from theories, for example the issue of how media violence might lead to violence in children. However, for this answer you need to give the issue (e.g. how children who watch violence on TV might become more aggressive, which is an important issue for society). 1 mark is usually for the issue itself; 2 further marks are available for saying more about it.
>
> **(15)** For this part of the question, you need to apply psychology to the issue you gave in (14). There are many ways of doing this and any useful contribution — where you link psychological understanding to the issue using the right approach — gains marks. You need to say quite a lot for 6 marks, and examples can be useful. You could aim to apply two or three concepts, for 3 marks, and gain the remaining 3 marks by saying more about them.
>
> **(16)** This is an essay question. 2 marks are for clarity and communication, gained by correct use of terms, good spelling and avoiding note form. 2 marks are for balance and breadth, gained by giving a good balance of AO1 (knowledge and understanding) and AO2 (evaluation and comment), as well as describing the issue briefly and applying concepts. This leaves 4 AO1 marks and 4 AO2 marks. 1 mark will be for the issue itself. The other marks are gained using material similar to that in (14) and (15) above, but don't spend too long outlining the issue. Spend time outlining the psychology and then be sure to evaluate and comment.

Answers to contemporary issue questions

(14) Media violence is a much-debated issue. ✓ The question is whether children who watch media violence become violent themselves. If this is the case, society should regulate what children watch. ✓ If it is found that media violence leads to aggression, we could consider showing pro-social behaviour to encourage that instead. ✓

> The issue is clear and outlined well. 1 mark is given for the issue, a further mark for why it is important (society must regulate) and a final mark for moving on to look at how showing pro-social behaviour might be useful. This is still part of the issue.

AS Psychology

(15) Social learning theory suggests that we learn by observation ✓ and studies such as those by Bandura show that when children watch aggressive acts, they are likely to imitate them. ✓ It has been shown that boys are more likely to imitate male models, and as 'TV villains' are often male, boys are likely to be more aggressive than girls. ✓ Also, if behaviour is rewarded, it is more likely to be imitated, which shows that there is an element of operant conditioning involved. ✓ Villains can be rewarded in TV programmes (even if only by enjoying the excitement) and this means that children are even more likely to imitate bad behaviour shown on television. ✓

> *e* This answer gives five clear points linking learning theory concepts to the issue of TV violence. To get the extra mark, more detail about research would be needed. The comments are too general, and adding empirical evidence (from studies) would elaborate and add depth to what is being said.

(16) One debate that frequently arises is whether or not violence portrayed on television leads to aggressive behaviour. Generally, the debate focuses on violence in children. If violence on television leads to real-life violence, then this is important for society. ✓ (AO1) There is already a nine o'clock watershed in place, which suggests that it is believed that aggression on television can lead to children being aggressive in reality. Those who conclude that violence on TV does lead to real-life violence propose that more prosocial behaviour be shown on television to encourage less violent behaviour. *Sesame Street* models this principle. Studies have indeed suggested that when aggression is modelled, children copy it. ✓ (AO1) Bandura et al. (1961) had adults model aggressive behaviour when they hit a bobo doll. There were different conditions, including using a male and a female adult. Then the researchers watched the children at play to see if the children who had watched the aggression would imitate it. They did — those children who had seen the adult hit the doll, also hit the doll when they were playing. Social learning theory suggests that children imitate models, as this study shows. ✓ (AO1) The boys tended to imitate the male model, which suggests that violent male actions on television will be copied by boys. Other studies have shown this too, such as a series of studies in Belgium and the USA where exciting films, including violence, were shown to some boys, and exciting films without violence to others. It was shown that those watching the aggressive TV tended to be more aggressive. ✓ (AO1) A problem with studies is that they tend to be experiments, which can be unnatural. The children in Bandura's study may have thought, having watched an adult hit a bobo doll, that they were supposed to hit the doll too. This would not be showing aggression, but obedience. ✓✓ (AO2) There may be little validity in such studies, so conclusions that children watching violent TV in their homes will then behave in an aggressive manner may not be warranted. The Belgium/USA series of studies is better because the films were shown in the boys' natural setting (they were in an institution) where films were shown in any case. This is likely to yield more valid data. ✓ (AO2) It has been claimed that violence on TV may lead to aggression in children, but there is more to it than that, such as whether aggression is also modelled in the family, for example. ✓ (AO2)

☒ This essay gets full marks. There is a good balance of describing the issue and the research involved and then making evaluative comments, so full balance and breadth marks are given. Terminology is used too, with good spelling and grammar, so full communication marks are awarded. The candidate has found 4 AO1 points and 4 AO2 points quite easily. He/she draws on two main studies only, but makes good use of them by describing them quite thoroughly and then evaluating both.

Section 2

AS Psychology

The psychodynamic approach

Key assumptions

(1) Outline *one* key assumption of the psychodynamic approach. (3 marks, AO1)
(2) Give *two* key assumptions of the psychodynamic approach. (2 marks, AO1)
(3) In the boxes below, tick the *two* statements that apply to the psychodynamic approach. (2 marks, AO1)

We develop through childhood through a series of stages, which are particularly important up to the age of 5 ☐
We develop through interactions with our environment; we experience stimuli and learn responses ☐
Our genetic make-up has a great influence on our development ☐
Reasons for our actions appear to come from conscious decision-making, but our unconscious has a large influence on us ☐

e **(1)** Say three things about a key assumption of this approach. 1 mark is likely to be for knowing the assumption (naming it), and 2 further marks for saying more about it. An example is a useful idea, but keep it short as it will not be worth 2 marks.

(2) Just naming two key assumptions is fine. You don't have to say more about them.

(3) Two ticks are required — no crosses. Put a tick against each of two statements that you think are correct.

Answers to key assumptions questions

(1) A great deal of our behaviour is motivated by unconscious wishes and desires that we repress. ✓ These thoughts are not conscious and cannot be accessed, which makes it very hard to know what is driving us. ✓ Defence mechanisms are used to keep unconscious forces from surfacing. ✓

e This answer is clearly expressed. It states a key assumption (unconscious forces are important) and then elaborates by saying what this means, mentioning repression and defence mechanisms. This is enough for the 3 marks.

(2) We are driven by unconscious forces, ✓ and the first 5 years of our lives are very important in developing our personality. ✓

e Although not a lot is said, two assumptions are clearly identified and so 2 marks are given.

(3) We develop through childhood through a series of stages, which are particularly important up to the age of 5 ✔

Edexcel Unit 2

We develop through interactions with our environment;
we experience stimuli and learn responses ☒
Our genetic make-up has a great influence on our development ☒
Reasons for our actions appear to come from conscious decision-making,
but our unconscious has a large influence on us ✓

> *e* The two ticks are in the right boxes. Although there are crosses in the other two boxes, it is quite clear that the candidate knows the right answer, so the marks are given. However, you should follow instructions carefully and avoid doing this.

■ ■ ■

Common research methods

(4) Give *one* strength and *one* weakness of case studies as a research method. (4 marks, AO2)

(5) Describe *one* research method that has commonly been used in the psychodynamic approach. (4 marks, AO1)

> *e* **(4)** There are two things to do and 4 marks available, in this case 2 marks for the strength and 2 for the weakness. Don't just give an answer for each: be sure to expand it enough for the full 2 marks. For example, say what a strength is, and then add more detail to explain it further.
>
> **(5)** 1 mark can be gained by naming or talking about a suitable research method. 3 further marks are available for describing the method. Remember that each point must be descriptive, not evaluative. For example, say what clinical interviews are and describe what happens, rather than mentioning how they might not be objective. This last point is an evaluative comment, which is not required for this question.

Answers to common research methods questions

(4) Case studies give lots of detail and specifics on the one participant, which means that in-depth data are gathered, and they are qualitative. ✓✓ A weakness is that they take a long time to do. ✓

> *e* The strength earns both marks as this one sentence makes several good points, i.e. 'lots of detail', 'specifics', 'on one participant', 'in-depth data' and 'qualitative'. This is easily enough for 2 marks. The weakness given is the time factor, which gains a mark, but it needs more for the second mark.

(5) Case studies are often used in the psychodynamic approach. ✓ One individual is studied in depth, delving into past experiences, particularly early years and relationships with parents. ✓ The study is done over a period of time, often in short sessions, ✓ and gradually, using different methods within the case study, a picture is built up both of an individual's function and of any past experiences that might

AS Psychology

affect that functioning. ✓ Qualitative data are gathered, but there can be subjectivity in interpretation.

e This is a clear description and there are more than 4 points made. Mentioning subjectivity does not gain a mark because it is comment rather than description. One strength of this answer is that it focuses on case studies as used in the approach. When describing research methods, think of them within the approach and make sure the focus is right.

■ ■ ■

In-depth areas of study

(6) Describe *one* theory in the psychodynamic approach other than Freud's. (5 marks, AO1)
(7) Outline *two* criticisms of a theory in the psychodynamic approach other than Freud's. (4 marks, AO2)
(8) Listed below are six terms used in the psychodynamic approach. Three are terms that Freud used to describe personality and the others are names of three of the psychosexual stages. Write in the box for each term 'P' if the term describes personality and 'S' if the term is a stage in psychosexual development.

| Oral ☐ | Id ☐ | Ego ☐ |
| Phallic ☐ | Superego ☐ | Anal ☐ | (3 marks, AO1)

e **(6)** You can choose which theory to describe as long as it is not Freud's and it is within the psychodynamic approach. 1 mark is usually for the theory itself, and 4 further marks are for description and detail. Remember not to evaluate — just say what the theory is about.

(7) There are two elements and 4 marks available, so 2 marks for each part. In each case 1 mark is for the criticism and a further mark is for saying more about it. Although you could argue that a critique involves positive as well as negative points, when a question asks for criticisms you should give negative points about the theory. Consider what it does not explain, or offer criticisms of the methods used to generate evidence for the theory.

(8) You need to write 'S' in three of the boxes, where the term is a stage, and 'P' in three of the boxes where the term is about personality. There are 3 marks — half a mark for each correct box. This is because once you have correctly identified three answers, the other three boxes can be completed without knowledge or understanding.

Answers to in-depth areas of study questions

(6) Piaget's theory is about stages in development; there are eight stages that a person goes through during their life. ✓ The first stage is when trust is gained and the last stage should be when they reach integrity. ✓

Edexcel Unit 2

> 🖉 It is tempting to think that this answer is wholly wrong as Piaget, who did have a stage theory, worked in the field of cognitive development. However, the theory appears to be Erikson's, so the wrong name is ignored and the first sentence has enough material (mentioning eight stages and a lifespan approach) to get at least 1 mark. The second mark comes from mentioning trust and integrity. If more had been said about each, 2 marks could have been given, but taking into account the original error, 1 seems fair here. More detail is needed for further marks.

(7) It is very hard to get evidence for Erikson's theory, as it is a lifespan theory mentioning concepts that are hard to test. Whether someone has reached a stage of generativity or not, for example, is quite hard to test, as the idea of generativity is hard to operationalise. ✓✓

> 🖉 This is a good answer, giving one clear criticism — that the concepts are hard to test. However, two criticisms are asked for, so only 2 marks out of 4 are awarded.

(8) Oral   S   Id   P   Ego   P
Phallic   S   Superego   P   Anal   S

> 🖉 Full marks are awarded. If one or two were wrong, the mark would be 2; three or four wrong would be 1 mark; five or six wrong would mean no marks.

■ ■ ■

Two studies

(9) Describe *one* study from the psychodynamic approach.   (5 marks, AO1)
(10) Evaluate *one* study from the psychodynamic approach.   (5 marks, AO2)
(11) Outline the findings of *two* studies from the psychodynamic approach.   (6 marks, AO1)

> 🖉 **(9)** Note that just describing what was done in the study (the procedure), or what was found (the results or findings), is not enough for all 5 marks. For the first mark, make sure the study is identifiable. A further mark can be gained by saying why the study was done, 2 more marks can be gained by saying what was done, and 2 more marks can be gained by saying what was found (the results). Marks can also be gained by giving the conclusion. Be sure to write enough, as for 5 marks you are trying to say five things.
>
> **(10)** Evaluation can come in many forms. You can give ethical issues (good and/or bad), alternative theories or studies, methodological problems (such as the reliability of experiments or the limitations of case studies), or criticisms of the study itself. Make sure you write enough for 5 marks. You are trying to say five things, although it is possible to gain more than 1 mark for a good, well-made point.
>
> **(11)** There are two tasks (the question is about two studies), so 3 marks are available for each. Note that only the findings/results are required, so do not describe the procedure of the study or the method. Focus on findings — you can give both the results and conclusions.

AS Psychology

Answers to two studies questions

(9) Freud's study of Little Hans was carried out to see if his phobia could be reduced. ✓ This was a case study. ✓

> There is just about enough for 2 marks here — 1 for the study itself and 1 for the aim and that it was a case study. However, there is no real description. The candidate should have added more detail, such as the fact that Hans was a 5-year-old boy, he had a fear of white horses and water, his dreams were analysed, and his father relayed all the information to Freud.

(10) The study of Little Hans can be criticised because Freud did not gather data directly but relied on the father's evidence. ✓ The parents were friends and followers of Freud, so they could have been looking out for things that Hans said and did that tied in with Freud's theories. ✓ This would mean that there was an element of subjectivity, both from the parents and from Freud himself. ✓

> This is a good, clear criticism. First, it is claimed that evidence is not direct. This point is elaborated for 2 more marks. For the remaining 2 marks, there needs to be another criticism, for instance pointing out how hard it is to replicate a case study like this, so its reliability is doubtful.

(11) Freud found evidence for the Oedipus complex in his study of Little Hans. ✓ Little Hans was afraid of white horses. It seemed that the horse could be a symbol for Little Hans's father, so Freud concluded that Hans's fear of horses represented his fear of his father. ✓✓ The findings from other case studies, such as the Rat Man, also show how ideas and fears can hide other unconscious desires. ✓

> The findings of the Little Hans study are outlined well and gain all 3 marks, but little is said about the Rat Man study, so only 1 mark is awarded. More detail is needed for the other 2 marks.

■ ■ ■

Key application

(12) Theories from the psychodynamic approach have helped to explain how mental health issues may be dealt with. Discuss how mental health issues are tackled by the psychodynamic approach. *(12 marks, essay)*

> **(12)** This is an essay question. 2 marks are for clarity and communication, gained by correct use of terms, good spelling and avoiding note form. 2 marks are for balance and breadth, gained by giving a good balance of AO1 (knowledge and understanding) and AO2 (evaluation and comment). This leaves 4 AO1 marks and 4 AO2 marks. You need to say four things about concepts in the psychodynamic approach that link to mental health and make four points in evaluation.

Answer to key application question

(12) Psychodynamic theory involves psychoanalysis, which is the main focus of the approach. The theory was developed from case studies that were carried out — their aim being to help individuals with mental health problems. One such case study was of 'Little Hans' who had a phobia which Freud helped to resolve by means of psychoanalysis. ✓ (AO1) The approach has the aim of helping those with mental illness, but also of helping us to maintain mental health. ✓ (AO2) It is thought that problems in early childhood lead to mental health problems. Early problems are repressed and defence mechanisms protect us by keeping problems in our unconscious. ✓ (AO1) However, energy is being used up in keeping problem thoughts in our unconscious, and using up energy in this way can lead to mental health problems such as anxiety, phobias, depression and obsessive–compulsive disorder. ✓ (AO1) It is by releasing problem thoughts from our unconscious by means of psychoanalysis — and making such thoughts conscious — that people can become mentally healthy. **(Maximum AO1 marks have already been achieved.)** However, other approaches have sought to explain mental disorders and might be seen as better explanations. For example, the learning approach suggests that phobias can be learnt through conditioning, and suggest that conditioning is a way of resolving phobias. Such treatment has been found to be successful, which suggests that the explanation may have merit too, and this opposes the psychodynamic explanation for phobias. ✓✓ (AO2) Similarly, depression can be helped by means of drug therapy, and this suggests that a cause could involve neurotransmitter functioning, which goes against the psychodynamic explanation. ✓ (AO2) Another problem with the psychodynamic explanation for mental health problems is that it is hard to test — the aspects of personality and concepts such as the Oedipus complex are not measurable and not easy to test. This has led many to reject the concepts entirely, although not being able to test something does not make it wrong. ✓ (AO2)

> There is a lot of good description and evaluation here. The approach is criticised by drawing on different explanations. This can be a successful way of evaluating, but take care not to describe a contrasting explanation too fully, as only 1 mark can be given for each contradicting piece of evidence. For example, 1 mark is for saying a learning explanation can help with phobias and 1 mark is for saying depression has an alternative explanation too. Even if more was said, more marks would be unlikely as the evaluation must focus on the psychodynamic approach itself. This answer gets the balance right, for full marks.

■ ■ ■

Contemporary issue

(13) The psychodynamic approach in psychology can be used to help us understand contemporary issues or debates. Describe *one* such contemporary issue or debate. *(4 marks, AO1)*

AS Psychology

section

(14) Using *two* concepts in the psychodynamic approach, explain how this approach can help us to understand the issue or debate that you outlined in question 13. (6 marks, AO2)

(15) Use your knowledge of the psychodynamic approach in psychology to describe and explain *one* contemporary issue or debate. (12 marks, essay)

> (13) You need to describe the issue briefly. Try to avoid applying theories if you can. Some issues are hard to separate from theories, for example the issue of recovered and false memories. 1 mark is usually for the issue itself, and 3 further marks are available for saying more about it.
>
> (14) Two concepts are required and there are 6 marks available, so 3 marks for each. You need to say three clear things or expand on a point in each case.
>
> (15) This is an essay question. 2 marks are for clarity and communication, gained by correct use of terms, good spelling and avoiding note form. 2 marks are for balance and breadth, gained by giving a good balance of AO1 (knowledge and understanding) and AO2 (evaluation and comment), as well as describing the issue briefly and applying concepts. This leaves 4 AO1 marks and 4 AO2 marks. 1 mark will be for the issue itself. The other marks are gained using material similar to that in (13) and (14) above. Don't spend too long outlining the issue; spend time outlining the psychology and then be sure to evaluate and comment.

Answers to contemporary issue questions

(13) A current issue that is really quite a new one is that of false-memory syndrome. ✓ The psychodynamic approach has long been interested in freeing repressed memories. This is seen as the way forward for the individual. ✓ However, following some reported cases where an individual has recalled early abuse only for it to be discovered that this was not the case, we now have what is called 'false-memory syndrome'. ✓ Families wrongly accused of abuse suffer terribly because of this; everyone becomes a victim. ✓

> 1 mark is given for the issue. A further mark is given for setting up the idea that recovering memories is the aim of psychoanalysis and another mark for showing that some recovered memories have been shown to be false. The final mark is given for highlighting the importance of the issue — that it can be traumatic for everyone. Although some theory is given here, for example about repressed memories needing to be recovered, this is part of the issue and helps to describe it, so is rewarded.

(14) The concept of the unconscious and how repressed wishes and desires affect decisions we make ✓ can help to explain why memories need to be recovered. It can explain false-memory syndrome to an extent, because the unconscious is, by definition, hard to access ✓ and so memories that seem to appear are not easily verified. ✓ Another concept is that of defence mechanisms. ✓ Defence mechanisms act to maintain thoughts in the unconscious so that they are not recovered. ✓ It is

hard to interpret when feelings are not real but represent hidden unconscious wishes, and this difficulty can lead to recovery of what are really false memories. ✓

> Two concepts are identified clearly and are awarded 1 mark each. The other 2 marks in each case are for saying what the concept is or means, and for linking it to false-memory syndrome.

(15) False-memory syndrome is a contemporary issue that has only recently been highlighted. During psychoanalysis, the aim is to discover repressed thoughts and wishes. By uncovering such thoughts, releasing them from the unconscious, and making them conscious, the individual should be able to deal with them. The thoughts will no longer be repressed, and energy will no longer be needed to keep them repressed, so the individual can release energy and be able to move on. ✓✓ (AO1) The problem is that it is not easy to uncover these unconscious thoughts and feelings. There are few ways of accessing the unconscious. The analyst can study the person's dreams, look for slips of the tongue, or try free association. However, these methods all involve interpretation by the analyst, and by the analysand. ✓ (AO1) It is this interpretation that can cause problems, and which has been said to lead to false-memory syndrome. ✓ (AO1) The analyst is focusing on certain areas of the person's life, mainly their early childhood and relationship with their parents. It is likely that these areas will be thoroughly explored. The Oedipus complex involves the resolution of conflicts involving both parents. When examining these conflicts, it is possible that issues such as abuse are seen in symbols. This abuse can of course be real. However, the element of interpretation and the role of symbols might lead to the conclusion that abuse has actually taken place when this memory is a false one. There have been cases where families have been accused of abuse but that has turned out to be false — the person being analysed has had a false memory uncovered. In some cases of analysis, hypnosis is used. An alternative explanation for false-memory syndrome is not that it is because of the interpretation of the analyst and patient, but that it comes directly from being hypnotised. ✓ (AO2) Some suggest that hypnosis is really social compliance and the person being hypnotised is likely to go along with suggestions of the hypnotist. This can lead to false memories. ✓ (AO2) It is not suggested that either a hypnotist or an analyst deliberately 'installs' a false memory — it is just that analysis can lead to this sort of memory being accepted, because it is in a way what is expected. ✓✓ (AO1)

> The essay clearly achieves full balance/breadth and communication marks. 1 mark is given for the issue too. The other 3 AO1 marks are clearly there — a lot of detail is given about the unconscious, repression and the role of psychoanalysis, as well as how this can lead to false memories. AO2 marks are harder to pick out as there is a lot of discussion in this essay. Clear AO2 marks are found in the discussion of hypnotism and how it can lead to false memories. There are other possible AO2 marks too, for example, where it is argued that abuse can be real but the element of interpretation means that false memories can indeed be found.

Section 3

The physiological approach

Key assumptions

(1) Outline *one* key assumption of the physiological approach. (3 marks, AO1)
(2) Give *two* key assumptions of the physiological approach. (2 marks, AO1)
(3) In the table below, tick the *two* statements that apply to the physiological approach. (2 marks, AO1)

The nervous system has an important role to play in our behaviour	☐
We develop through interactions with our environment; we experience stimuli and learn responses	☐
Our genetic make-up has a great influence on our development	☐
Reasons for our actions appear to come from conscious decision-making, but our unconscious has a large influence on us	☐

e **(1)** Say three things about a key assumption of this approach. 1 mark is likely to be for knowing the assumption (naming it), and 2 marks for saying more about it. An example is a useful idea, but keep it short as it will not be worth 2 marks.

(2) Just naming two key assumptions is fine. You don't have to say more about them.

(3) Two ticks are required — no crosses. Put a tick against each of two statements that you think are correct.

Answers to key assumptions questions

(1) The importance of genes and of the nervous system. ✓

e Two assumptions are given but neither is outlined, so only 1 mark is awarded overall.

(2) The importance of genes ✓ and of the nervous system ✓ when looking for reasons for our behaviour and other characteristics.

e 1 mark is awarded for each assumption, so full marks. They only need to be identifiable as assumptions.

(3)

The nervous system has an important role to play in our behaviour	✔
We develop through interactions with our environment; we experience stimuli and learn responses	✔
Our genetic make-up has a great influence on our development	✔
Reasons for our actions appear to come from conscious decision-making, but our unconscious has a large influence on us	☐

e Although this candidate has identified two correct statement (about the nervous system and about genetic makeup), there is a third tick. No marks are awarded, as the candidate might have been hedging his/her bets.

Edexcel Unit 2

Common research methods

(4) Give *one* strength and *one* weakness of using correlational techniques as a research method. (4 marks, AO2)

(5) Describe *one* research method commonly used in the physiological approach. (4 marks, AO1)

> *e* **(4)** There are two things to do and 4 marks are available, in this case 2 marks for the strength and 2 for the weakness. Don't just give an answer for each; be sure to expand it enough for the full 2 marks. For example, say what a strength is and then add more detail to explain it further.
>
> **(5)** 1 mark would be gained by naming or talking about a suitable research method. 3 further marks are available for describing the method. Remember that each point must be descriptive, not evaluative. For example, say what correlations are and describe what happens, rather than mentioning that they do not prove cause and effect. This last point is an evaluative comment, which is not required.

Answers to common research methods questions

(4) One strength of a correlation is that there is often no direct manipulation of an IV, so what is measured can often be more natural than in experiments. For example, if looking at whether both identical twins have schizophrenia, the variable (having schizophrenia or not, and being identical twins) would have to be naturally occurring. ✓✓ A weakness is that although variables can be identified as being linked or not, there is no cause-and-effect relationship. ✓

> *e* The strength is explained enough for 2 marks, but the weakness needs more detail to show clear understanding and is awarded 1 mark.

(5) One method used is an EEG to measure brain activity. ✓ Electrodes are attached to the scalp. ✓ A computer image shows the pattern of brain waves. ✓

> *e* 1 mark is given for the research method (EEG), 1 mark for saying that electrodes are attached to the scalp and a further mark for saying what is seen as a result. The final mark could be gained by saying that this is a non-invasive method and that it is used to measure sleep patterns.

■ ■ ■

In-depth areas of study

(6) What is a zeitgeber? (1 mark, AO1)
(7) Describe *one* physiological theory of dreaming. (4 marks, AO1)
(8) Evaluate a *physiological* theory of dreaming in terms of *one* strength and *one* weakness. (4 marks, AO2)

> *e* **(6)** There is only 1 mark available, so just give a definition of zeitgeber. You can use an example to illustrate the definition, but this alone is not enough.

AS Psychology

(7) 1 mark is usually for the theory itself and 3 further marks are available for descriptive points about it. Remember not to evaluate — don't comment on what is good or bad about the theory, just say what it is about.

(8) There are two tasks, and 4 marks available, so 2 marks are for the strength and 2 marks for the weakness. There is 1 mark each for the strength and weakness, and in each case a further mark for elaboration. Note that the word 'physiological' is emphasised to remind you not to give Freud's theory, for example.

Answers to in-depth areas of study questions

(6) A time-keeper, for example food at regular times. ✓

e This answer is clear because time-keeper is correct (although the candidate could be thinking of an internal mechanism); adding the part about food makes it clearer. This is an illustration of how giving an example can help to show that you know the answer.

(7) One physiological theory of dreaming suggests that nerve impulses turn into random thoughts and link together to make a story. ✓ Our thoughts in dreams are unclear as the brain can't link them. ✓ This is Hobson and McCarley's activation–synthesis theory. ✓

e 1 mark is given for naming an appropriate theory. A further mark is awarded for the idea of random neuronal firing and another for the lack of clarity of dreams. However, this is not very clearly described and a little more detail is needed for the final mark.

(8) The activation–synthesis model explains why dreams can be odd and not easy to understand. ✓ A weakness is that the theory does not explain why we dream of past experiences. ✓

e 1 mark is awarded here for the strength and 1 mark for the weakness but both need elaboration for the other 2 marks. For example, as well as saying dreams are not easy to understand, the candidate could say that this is because there is random firing and different 'thoughts' will be triggered, which will be hard to make sense of. For the weakness, the candidate could add that people often report dreams that include something about a television programme they watched the night before, or about previous occurrences, and this cannot be explained by random firing of neurones.

■ ■ ■

Two studies

(9) Describe *one* study from the physiological approach. (5 marks, AO1)
(10) Evaluate *one* study from the physiological approach. (5 marks, AO2)
(11) Outline the procedures of *two* studies from the physiological approach. (6 marks, AO1)

Edexcel Unit 2

(9) Note that just describing what was done in the study (the procedure), or what was found (the results or findings), is not enough for all 5 marks. For the first mark, make sure the study is identifiable. 1 further mark can be gained by saying what the study was done for. 2 marks can be gained by saying what was done and 2 more marks can be gained by saying what was found (the results). Marks can also be gained by giving the conclusion. There are more ways than one to get the 5 marks. Be sure to write enough, as for 5 marks you are trying to say five things.

(10) Evaluation can come in many forms. You can give ethical issues (good and/or bad), alternative theories or studies, methodological problems (such as the reliability of experiments or the limitations of case studies), or criticisms of the study itself. Make sure you write enough for 5 marks. You are trying to say five things, although it is possible to gain more than 1 mark for a good, well-made point.

(11) There are two tasks (the question is about two studies), so 3 marks are available for each. Note that only the procedures are required, so do not describe the findings of the study, or the method. Focus on what was done.

Answers to two studies questions

(9) A study on rats was carried out to see what would happen if they were not allowed to sleep. ✓ The rats that could not sleep died but a control group of rats that were allowed to sleep did not die. ✓

This is the Rechtschaffen et al. (1983) study. 2 marks are awarded for the aim and the findings. The study is not fully identified by the candidate, so no mark is given for the study itself. The procedure needs to be outlined, as anyone reading this would not know what was done in the study.

(10) Findings from the Rechtschaffen study are applied to humans and it is said that being deprived of sleep is harmful. However, generalising findings from animal studies to humans is perhaps not straightforward as there are differences between animals and humans. ✓✓ However, the study was replicated, so it is reliable. ✓ It has been said that as well as being deprived of sleep the rats were stimulated, so this might have been a confounding factor. ✓

The point about difficulty in generalising gains 2 marks because it is set up by explaining the study briefly and then justified by giving a reason (that there are differences). It is a good point to say that the study is reliable because it was replicated (try to avoid just saying a study is reliable — say why), for another mark. The fourth mark is given for mentioning the possible confounding factor. Elaboration of this point could have gained another mark.

(11) One study was done by Rechtschaffen et al. (1983). They set up apparatus so that a rat was on a disc surrounded by water. ✓ An EEG measured the rat's brain patterns. ✓ For the experimental condition, when the rat could be seen

AS Psychology

to be asleep (using brain patterns), the disc was slowly rotated, making the rat walk with the disc (or it would have fallen into the water). ✓ This had the effect of keeping the rat awake. Another study was done by Dement and Kleitman (1957). They woke people during REM sleep to see whether they were dreaming. ✓ They also watched the direction of eye movements during REM and then asked about dreams to see if the direction of movement matched the content of the dream. ✓ They also looked at the timing of REM sleep. The method was observation (e.g. of eye movements) and interview (to find out about content of dreams). ✓

> This answer is quite thorough. Knowing the two studies is creditable, and enough information is given about the procedure to get the full 3 marks in each case. The ticks represent marking points but credit could have been given in other places. 1 mark could have been given for each study — this would be decided in advance and written into the mark scheme. Don't rely on getting marks for the study, but make sure you describe the procedure in enough detail for the full marks.

Key application

(12) Read the source below. Then explain what is being said, using concepts from the physiological approach. *(6 marks, AO2)*

Source

John works shifts at a local factory, and is looking for a '9 to 5' job instead. He has a young family and he finds it very hard to sleep during the day, because the children naturally make quite a bit of noise. Also, he cannot join a quiz team with his mates, as he changes shift every week. As soon as he gets used to nights a bit, he finds that he has to swap to evenings, and then for the week after he works days. He feels tired most of the time, and has had a number of bouts of flu and stomach upsets. He thinks that his job is making him ill.

(13) Studies and theories within the physiological approach have been applied when looking at problems with shiftwork. Discuss the application of the physiological approach to help those on shiftwork. *(12 marks, essay)*

> **(12)** There are 6 marks available, so either give six different points or give three different points with elaboration, or two points with more detailed elaboration. Mention the source at least once and then use any concepts from the physiological approach to shed light on John's situation.
>
> **(13)** This is an essay question. 2 marks are for clarity and communication, gained by correct use of terms, good spelling, and avoiding note form. 2 marks are for balance and breadth, gained by giving a good balance of AO1 (knowledge and understanding) and AO2 (evaluation and comment), as well as briefly describing the issue and applying concepts. This leaves 4 AO1 marks and 4 AO2 marks. The AO1 marks are gained by showing knowledge and understanding of research into shiftwork; the AO2 marks are gained by evaluating this research.

Answers to key application questions

(12) The source emphasises how John is having problems sleeping during the day and working at night. His sleep is disrupted during the day. Knowing about circadian rhythms can help to explain the problems. ✓ We have an internal body clock that works to something like a 25-hour cycle, as Siffre's study showed. ✓ Zeitgebers keep this to a 24-hour cycle and daylight and darkness are powerful zeitgebers. ✓

> *e* This is a reasonable answer, but does not give enough for 6 marks. One strength is that the candidate refers to the source, which is necessary. A mark is given for setting the scene and mentioning circadian rhythms. Another mark is given for the Siffre findings and a third mark for linking these to the need for zeitgebers. The answer needs to show that shiftwork gives the wrong zeitgebers, as John is trying to sleep during daylight hours. Even the household noises will be the wrong zeitgebers. Other possible points include mentioning that altering temperature rhythms is harder than altering other rhythms, so he is likely to feel tired and unwell.

(13) Shiftwork generally involves rotating through three different shifts, often one per week. Some people, though, are on permanent nights. It appears that sleeping at different times of the day and changing shifts affects people and makes them unwell. Some accidents have happened in the early hours, and it has been suggested that this is due to unnatural sleeping patterns or changing shifts. We have more than one internal body clock and sleep, temperature and metabolic rate are some of the rhythms that change during a 24-hour (circadian) cycle. External cues called zeitgebers help to regulate our circadian rhythms. If we are constantly changing shifts, zeitgebers are not going to be appropriate; for example, we will have to sleep during daylight hours. Also, our different bodily rhythms can get out of step as some rhythms adjust more easily than others. Some people adjust more easily than others too, so perhaps they are better at working shifts than others, or at least it affects them less. ✓ (AO1)

> *e* At first sight, this seems to be a good essay but it does not answer the question. The candidate uses concepts from the physiological approach to explain problems with shiftwork but does not address how findings from the approach can be used to help those who work in shifts. The final point, that some are better suited to shiftwork than others, implies that we should try to ensure that those not suited do not do it, so a mark is given. The use of terms and communication skills are good enough for 2 marks. 1 balance and breadth mark is also given as, although by no means completely irrelevant, the answer does not focus well on the question. The candidate needs to give the findings that show that we should rotate shifts forwards not back, and suggest that weekly shift changes are not useful; they should change approximately once every 3 weeks. Zeitgebers could be used, in that bright lighting might help workers. These are the sorts of comments needed.

section 3

AS Psychology

Contemporary issue

(14) Outline *one* contemporary issue or debate that can be explained using the physiological approach. (3 marks, AO1)

(15) Explain how the physiological approach can help us to understand this issue or debate. (6 marks, AO2)

(16) Use your knowledge of the physiological approach in psychology to describe and explain *one* contemporary issue or debate. (12 marks, essay)

(14) You need to outline the issue briefly. Try to avoid applying theories if you can. Some issues are hard to separate from theories, for example the 24-hour society. 1 mark is usually for the issue itself and 2 further marks are available for saying more about it.

(15) For this part of the question you need to apply psychology to the issue you gave in question 14. There are many ways of doing this and any useful contribution — where you link psychological understanding to the issue, using the right approach — gains marks. You need to say quite a lot for 6 marks and examples can be useful. You could aim to apply two or three concepts for 3 marks and earn the remaining 3 marks by saying more about them.

(16) This is an essay question. 2 marks are for clarity and communication, gained by correct use of terms, good spelling and avoiding note form. 2 marks are for balance and breadth, gained by giving a good balance of AO1 (knowledge and understanding) and AO2 (evaluation and comment), as well as describing the issue briefly and applying concepts. This leaves 4 AO1 marks and 4 AO2 marks. 1 mark is for the issue itself. The other marks are gained using material similar to that in (14) and (15), but don't spend too long outlining the issue. Spend time outlining the psychology and then be sure to evaluate and comment.

Answers to contemporary issue questions

(14) Narcolepsy is a condition in which an individual can suddenly fall asleep, ✓ often after meals or in the afternoon. ✓ Sufferers are often aged between 15 and 25 years old, and more men suffer from narcolepsy than women. ✓ Narcolepsy sufferers cannot drive because they may suddenly fall asleep. It is not dangerous in itself but can have dangerous consequences.

1 mark is given for the issue (narcolepsy), and another mark for mentioning that it can happen at particular times. A further mark is given for mentioning the typical age and gender of sufferers. Another mark could be given for mentioning possible consequences; however, this is not necessary as maximum marks have already been awarded.

(15) Narcolepsy seems to be genetic, although the cause is not known. It is hard to see how environmental factors could cause narcolepsy. ✓ It can be treated with drugs, including caffeine. Messages are passed in the brain by means of neurotrans-

Edexcel Unit 2

mitters and drugs affect neurotransmitters, so if drugs help with narcolepsy, we can suggest that there is a problem with neurotransmitters and the brain's communication. ✓✓ EEG patterns are investigated to see what causes the sudden falling asleep. ✓

e Marks are gained here for bringing in the nature/nurture debate when looking for a cause for narcolepsy, and for discussing the role of neurotransmitters and drug treatments. The first mark could almost be a double mark, as both nature and nurture are mentioned, but there is not quite enough detail for 2 marks. However, the second point gets 2 marks because there is quite a bit of information. The final mark is for discussing EEG measures. These concepts (genes, neurotransmitters and EEG) are all clearly from the physiological approach, demonstrating that the candidate has focused on the question. The other 2 marks could have been gained by looking more at drugs. For example, amphetamines and caffeine seem to help and these are drugs that stimulate the brain, so narcolepsy might be caused by some loss of stimulation. Also, antidepressants help with cataplexy (when the head slumps and the knees buckle), which tends to go with narcolepsy.

(16) A link has been made between intelligence and genetics — whether or not intelligence is inherited. ✓ (AO1) This is part of a debate about whether traits are due to nature or nurture. ✓ (AO1) Evidence for the idea that IQ is genetic includes twin studies, which show that IQ levels are similar in mz twins. ✓ (AO1) These are identical twins; they share 100% of their genes. Even when identical twins are raised in different environments, their IQ scores tend to be similar, which suggests that IQ is genetic. ✓ (AO2) However, environment also plays a role in intelligence. ✓ (AO2) Adoption studies have shown that children from deprived backgrounds and who have relatively low IQ scores show an increase in IQ score if adopted into families with a more stimulating environment. ✓ (AO1) As these children have no genetic connection with the new family, this suggests that environment plays a role. ✓ (AO2) It is likely that people have a basic intelligence that they are born with and this becomes shaped by environment, upbringing and standard of education. ✓ (AO2)

e This essay is awarded full marks. AO1 marks are given for knowledge and understanding but often what is knowledge in this essay is also given as comment. For example, 'even when identical twins are raised in different environments, their IQ scores tend to be similar', is an AO1 point, but adding 'which suggests that IQ is genetic' makes it a comment. There is sufficient material here for all 8 marks (AO1 and AO2). Often an examiner will note that a sentence or point could be either AO1 or AO2 and will allocate marks in the way that gives the candidate the best mark.